Across Frontiers

across Frontiers

Hispanic Crafts of New Mexico

By Dexter Cirillo
In collaboration with Nancy Pletka Benkof

Photographs by Eric Swanson

CHRONICLE BOOKS
SAN FRANCISCO

for

DENNIS PAUL CIRILLO

Text copyright ©1998 by Dexter Cirillo.
Photographs copyright ©1998 by Eric Swanson.
All rights reserved. No part of this book may
be reproduced in any form without written
permission from the publisher.

Library of Congress Cataloging-in-Publication
Data available.

ISBN 0-8118-1774-1 (pbk)
      0-8118-1793-8 (hc)

Printed in Hong Kong.

Book + cover design by Joseph Stitzlein ~ SF, CA

Distributed in Canada by Raincoast Books
8680 Cambie Street
Vancouver, British Columbia V6P 6M9

10 9 8 7 6 5 4 3 2 1

Chronicle Books
85 Second Street
San Francisco, California 94105

Web Site: www.chronbooks.com

Page 4:
A view of Las Trampas, 1910.
Founded in 1754, Las Trampas
translates as "traps," referring
to the snares trappers used to
capture animals.

Images from frontmatter -

Page 2:
This nineteenth-century band-and-
stripe Rio Grande weaving has
smaller than usual stripes incorporated into the bands. The dyes
are brazilwood and indigo.

Page 3:
The workbench for Santero
Félix López holds some of the
hand tools and files he uses
to carve in the features of his
bultos (sculptures).

Images from Table of Contents -
(clockwise from top left)

Todas las Madres is a weaving
Lisa Trujillo began when
her mother-in-law was dying.
"I wanted to explore mother-
hood," she says, "and I picked
the pattern of the bow because
bows are maternal, and they
also show how everything
is connected."

Lawrence Quintana has transformed a utilitarian two-wheeled
cart into a work of art, embell-
ishing the frame and wheels
with elaborate chip-carving and
floral and geometric designs in
the style of José Dolores López.
On the wheels, Quintana
has added a figure that can

be variously interpreted
as an angel, a dove, or an eagle—
also inspired by José Dolores
López.

Vicki Rodríguez is known for
the intricacy of her floral designs,
created from hundreds of finely
cut slivers of straw. She learned
appliqué from her parents,
Paula and Eliseo Rodríguez,
and like them she also portrays
the santos in straw appliqué.

This kneeling of St. Jerome
is one of nine figures from
Marie Romero Cash's altar
screen (see page 135). St. Jerome
is the subject of an apocryphal
story in which he removed a
thorn from a lion's paw.

Table of Contents

1
Hispanic Weaving of the Rio Grande
p.26

2
Woodworking and Furniture Making
p.58

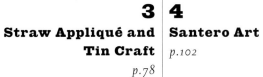

3
Straw Appliqué and Tin Craft
p.78

4
Santero Art
p.102

Preface and Acknowledgments

N 1992, NANCY PLETKA BENKOF PROPOSED the subject of this book to me. A collector and champion of contemporary Hispanic art, she saw a vacuum that needed to be filled. No one had written a book that encompassed the contemporary expression of all the Spanish art traditions that had grown out of New Mexico's four-hundred-year history: textiles, furniture, decorative arts, and religious art. While excellent books had been written on the historic arts produced during the Spanish Colonial (1598–1821), Mexican (1821–1846), and Territorial (1846–1912) periods, and others had covered the WPA era of federally funded arts projects in New Mexico, much of the twentieth century had been ignored. Yet, the number of artists participating in Santa Fe's annual Spanish Market had multiplied more than eight times since it was reinstated in 1965, matched by a receptive audience of collectors, galleries, and museums. At Nancy's suggestion, the Heard Museum in Phoenix mounted a successful show of contemporary Hispanic art in 1992 entitled *CHISPAS! Cultural Warriors of New Mexico*. *Chispas* can be translated as "spark" or tiny diamond, and that show and its catalogue were the spark that ignited Nancy's commitment to pursuing a book on contemporary art.

The subject of Spanish art traditions of New Mexico chimed with my own interests and some of my background. I had first visited New Mexico in 1965, when I trained for the Peace Corps at the University of New Mexico. I spent the next two years in Colombia, South America, an experience that opened the door for me to lead study groups to Mexico and Spain, acquainting me with the history of those countries. I returned to New Mexico many times over the years for various projects, one of which culminated in the 1992 publication of my last book, *Southwestern Indian Jewelry*. During several of my research trips to New Mexico, I stayed with Nancy and her husband, Paul Pletka, and was introduced by them to the traditional Hispanic arts of New Mexico. With Nancy, I interviewed a number of artists in 1992, attended the summer and winter Spanish Markets over the next couple of years, and Easter Week services in Córdova one year—all the time reading more about the history of New Mexico. Despite my interest in the region and Nancy's devotion to the arts, however, we needed to find a reason for the book beyond its documentation of a contemporary art movement.

Why has this art lasted four hundred years? What does it represent? And why is it so appealing to people from all kinds of backgrounds in the late twentieth century?

The answer, I think, can be found in values that, unfortunately, are rapidly diminishing in our postmodern age of communications: values of family and community, spiritual certitude, respect for tradition and history, and a commitment to process. In an era when Americans are constantly changing their addresses, it's remarkable to witness a culture that has been regionally intact for four centuries. That continuity is exactly what has created a history and a parade of traditions that New Mexico's Hispanic population has handed down from one generation to the next. Agueda Martínez, for example, at age ninety-eight, still weaves every day and has devoted her life to teaching dozens of members of her own family and others the skills required to produce the stunning textiles of the Rio Grande tradition.

Doña Agueda's art is not folk art, though she is an unpretentious person of modest means. Rather, her art is the result of years of daily practice, of knowing which plants will yield the truest colors, of carding and spinning her own yarn when time allows, of warping the loom, of simply weaving. For her, the process is the art, as it is for the *santero* (a maker of religious images), who splits the wood, carves an image, prepares the gesso to cover the wood, grinds pigments for paints, and finally executes the painting. The steps involved for all the arts in this book require discipline, knowledge, and a commitment to process. While these are criteria for any act of creation, for the Hispanic artist the process also links the past to the present. From a historic perspective, art is a family affair.

This is not to say that contemporary Hispanic art is static or a mirror image of the past: quite the opposite. The arts would not sustain themselves, nor would they hold our attention, were it not for the vitality and vision that New Mexican artists of the 1990s bring to their history. Their interpretation of the traditions of their ancestors through the filter of their own experience has yielded an art that is genuine and innovative.

This is also a book about religious faith—a subject that has become irrelevant to many people in our culture as we embark on the twenty-first century. Spiritual devotion inspires much of the work presented here, whether it is the panoply of religious images created by the santeros, the straw appliquéd biblical scenes on crosses, or the tin nichos for saints. There is an authenticity of expression that comes from such faith, and perhaps it is that inexplicable connection to a greater purpose that attracts our attention. Or perhaps it is the comfort this art provides to its creators, confident of their past, that spills over to us, reminding us of our own evanescent ties to family and tradition.

§

In 1996, four years after Nancy proposed this subject to me, I signed a contract with Chronicle Books to write *Across Frontiers*. Nancy agreed to collaborate with me, and together we outlined the general direction of the book and the artists to be included. In the fall and winter of 1996–1997, I sent questionnaires to the more than eighty artists in the book and arranged personal and telephone interviews with many of them over the ensuing months. Nancy's friendship with the artists opened many doors and made my research a pure pleasure. She selected the art for the book, though we discussed and agreed on each piece, and she assumed the Herculean task of coordinating the photography. Given the number of artists and the dozens of objects to be gathered from museums, private collectors, galleries, and artists, this was invaluable, freeing me to concentrate on my interviews, research, and writing.

Many people have contributed their knowledge and goodwill to this project, and I would like to begin by thanking the artists for their generosity of spirit and warm reception of Nancy and myself. Our hardest task has been to omit many deserving artists because of space restrictions. Their excellence, we know, will be acknowledged in future works.

The book would not exist without the superlative skill and dedication of our photographer, Eric Swanson. He juggled a busy schedule (sometimes upon a moment's notice) from October 1996 to May 1997 to photograph the art, the studios, and the location shots, sometimes returning to redo shots because of bad weather or simply for his own sense of perfection. I am grateful for his professionalism and aesthetic vision, which have made this book as beautiful as it is.

Across Frontiers covers four centuries. I could not have summarized this history, however so briefly, without the inestimable scholarship of the works listed in the bibliography. Of those, I would especially like to acknowledge the following authors:

In the introduction, I am indebted to Marc Simmons for his entertaining and accomplished biography of Juan de Oñate in *The Last Conquistador—Juan de Oñate and the Settling of the Far Southwest.*

Chapter 1 on Hispanic weaving would not be possible without the comprehensive history provided in *Spanish Textile Tradition of New Mexico and Colorado,* edited by Nora Fisher. The new edition of that book, *Rio Grande Textiles,* contains an excellent introduction by Teresa Archuleta-Sagel that is especially enlightening on contemporary weaving. Don Usner has captured the charm and the history of Chimayó in *Sabino's Map,* offering insights into the early commercialization of the Chimayó weavings.

The 1996 publication of *Spanish New Mexico,* edited by Donna Pierce and Marta Weigle, has been an important contribution to the field. Donna Pierce's essay on Spanish Colonial furniture in this two-volume work documents the evolution of furniture styles from Spain to the New World. In chapter 2, I am indebted to her for her impeccable research. I would also like to acknowledge the exceptional scholarship of Lonn Taylor and Dessa Bokides in *New Mexican Furniture—1600–1940.*

Lane Coulter and Maurice Dixon's *New Mexican Tinwork—1840–1940*—with its comprehensive survey of the history and styles of New Mexican tinwork—was an invaluable resource for chapter 3. I am grateful as well to Donna Pierce for her illuminating essays on straw appliqué and tinwork in *Spanish New Mexico.*

Throughout my research, E. Boyd's seminal work, *Popular Arts of Spanish New Mexico,* has been helpful, but especially so for chapter 4 on santero art. Robin Gavin's *Traditional Arts of Spanish New Mexico* provides an excellent overview of Spanish Colonial santero art. For her groundbreaking work on the Penitente Brotherhood in *Brothers of Light, Brothers of Blood,* I thank Marta Weigle. Similarly, William Wroth's remarkable *Images of Penance, Images of Mercy* places New Mexican penitential art within the long history of European Catholicism. For the background information on José Dolores López and his descendants, I would like to thank Charles Briggs for his intelligent book, *The Wood Carvers of Córdova, New Mexico.* In *Built of Earth and Song—Churches of Northern New Mexico,* Marie Romero Cash provides a much-needed service in describing the religious art in various churches. My deepest gratitude goes to Thomas J. Steele for *Santos and Saints—The Religious Folk Art of Hispanic New Mexico,* a book of superior scholarship that places New Mexican santero art within the contexts of European art as well as Catholic history.

I also thank the following directors and staffs of the museums for their warm cooperation in letting us photograph objects from their collections: at the Museum of International Folk Art in Santa Fe, Charlene Cerny (director), Robin Gavin (curator), and Mariah Sacoman (former curator of Southwestern Hispanic folk art); at the Taylor Museum of the Colorado Springs Fine Arts Center, Cathy Wright (director and chief curator); at the Albuquerque Museum, Ellen J. Landis (curator); at El Rancho de las Golondrinas Museum in Santa Fe, Donna Pierce (curator); and at the Millicent Rogers Museum in Taos, David Revere McFadden (former director) and Guadalupe Tafoya (curator).

I am also most appreciative of the efforts of Arthur L. Olivas, photographic archivist for the Museum of New Mexico, in helping me find archival photographs that document the historic arts and churches of New Mexico. And to Father Edmund Savilla of Our Lady of Guadalupe Church in Taos; Marina Ochoa, director of the archdiocese of Santa Fe; and Father Leo Lucero, pastor of Cristo Rey Church in Santa Fe, I am grateful for their cooperation and the commissions the archdiocese has given to Hispanic artists.

Of the many collectors who opened their homes to us, I would especially like to acknowledge Ray and Judy Dewey for their patronage of Hispanic artists in their own collecting and in promoting contemporary Hispanic art through shows at Dewey Galleries, Ltd., beginning in the 1970s. My appreciation also goes to Barbara Douglas for sharing her collection with us and for introducing us to collectors in Albuquerque.

I thank as well the following people for generously giving their time to read the manuscript under the pressure of deadlines and for their discerning comments, which I hope I have interpreted correctly: Robin Gavin and Marie Romero Cash (introduction); Teresa Archuleta-Sagel (chapter 1); Donna Pierce (chapter 2); Marie Romero Cash (chapter 3); Charles Carrillo, Félix López, and Thomas J. Steele (chapter 4); Nancy Pletka Benkof, who read the entire manuscript in all its versions; and Eric Lax, who has read this and all my previous works with good humor and pertinent suggestions.

I owe a big thanks to Emily Miller, formerly at Chronicle Books, for believing in the project; to Edward Weidenfeld for putting it together; and to Jay Schaefer, my editor, for shaping it into a harmonious whole.

And finally, as always, I thank my husband, Dennis, for enduring yet another tight schedule, and for his love.

~ *Dexter Cirillo* ~

Introduction

LOCATED ON A HIGH DESERT PLATEAU BETWEEN the Rio Grande and the Sangre de Cristo Mountains, the villages of Chimayó, Córdova, Truchas, Las Trampas, Chamisal, Peñasco, Vadito, and Talpa spread out like beads on a rosary along the high road from Santa Fe to Taos. These are the villages of the "Rio Arriba," the northern watershed of the Rio Grande, colonized by the Spanish over a period of two and a half centuries before New Mexico became an American territory in 1846.

Of these villages, Chimayó has, perhaps, become the most well known to people outside northern New Mexico because of El Santuario de Nuestro Señor de Esquípulas, a shrine renowned for the mysterious healing powers of its sacred dirt and a crucifix of the Christ of Esquípulas. According to oral history, Don Bernardo Abeyta discovered the crucifix under miraculous circumstances and petitioned the church in 1813 for permission to build a chapel dedicated to Esquípulas in Potrero just outside of Chimayó. Completed in 1816, the Santuario was erected on ground considered hallowed by the Tewa Indians for centuries because of its magic curative powers. They would mix the earth with water and ingest it or apply it for medicinal purposes. A small room was built next to the sacristy to house the well of healing earth, *el posito,* where it exists today, attracting thousands of pilgrims to the Santuario each year, especially during Easter Week.

Next to the Santuario is the Chapel of El Santo Niño de Atocha, which was built by Severiano Medina in 1857, a year after Abeyta died. Medina attributed his extraordinary recovery from a fatal illness to his prayers to the Santo Niño. The popular version of El Santo Niño de Atocha recounts a battle between the Moors and the Christians in medieval Spain in which many Spanish Christians were imprisoned in the town of Atocha. They were denied visits by family members, who sought to bring them food and water. Fearful that their husbands and sons would die, the women of the village prayed for help. A child dressed as a pilgrim, carrying a basket of food and a gourd of water at the end of a staff, appeared at the prison gates and was allowed to enter. When he left, after having fed all of the prisoners, his basket and gourd were still full. To the prisoners and their families, the child was Jesus Christ incarnate, who had answered their prayers and come to save them.

A view of the austere New Mexican landscape outside Chimayó, interrupted by a single white cross.

El Santuario de Nuestro Señor de Esquípulas, built by Bernardo Abeyta in Potrero near Chimayó and popularly known as Santuario de Chimayó, ca. 1915–1917. Abeyta's choice to honor Nuestro Señor de Esquípulas, who was unknown to New Mexicans in the early nineteenth century, was apparently based on reports he may have heard in his travels to northern Mexico of a similar shrine built in 1578 in the town of Esquípulas, Guatemala, in which a crucifix of the "Black Christ" was worshipped and where the earth was also associated with mysterious recuperative powers. The "Black Christ" was so named because the crucifix was carved from a dark brown wood.

The faith that led Bernardo Abeyta and Severiano Medina to build family chapels to express their devotion is the same faith that sustained the Spanish colonizers of the Southwest over two hundred years earlier when they followed Juan de Oñate into New Mexico in 1598. Francisco Vásquez de Coronado had led a massive expedition into New Mexico in 1540–1542, pushing northward from Mexico, or New Spain as it was then called, to explore the frontier regions that would become the state of New Mexico in 1912. Franciscan missionaries accompanied both expeditions of Coronado and Oñate, establishing between forty-five and fifty churches in New Mexico by 1660 and fulfilling a mandate set forth by the Spanish Crown in the 1573 Laws of the Indies to spread Christianity to the New World.

Oñate's journey covered more than six hundred miles and took six months to complete, expanding the Camino Real from Mexico City into northern New Mexico to almost two thousand miles. In exchange for funding the expedition and providing food, clothing, tools, and livestock (reportedly seven thousand head of cattle, oxen, goats, horses, mules, donkeys, and sheep) for his some two hundred soldier/settlers and family members, Oñate was appointed governor of the New Mexico territory.

Oñate's choice to locate the first capital of New Mexico at San Juan de Los Caballeros, near the San Juan Pueblo north of Santa Fe, was based on several factors: the Española valley was fertile and well suited for agriculture; the neighboring Tewa Indians were reported to be friendly and possessed of large stores of food for the winter; and the central location allowed the more ambitious of Oñate's party to venture into the nearby Sangre de Cristo mountain range in search of silver and the elusive gold that Coronado had so desperately hoped to discover at the Zuni Pueblos almost sixty years earlier. Moreover, the stark landscape of northern New Mexico, with its rounded hills dotted with piñon and juniper and the red and ochre colors of the high desert, reminded the settlers of their native Extremadura region in Spain.

In 1608, the Franciscan missionaries baptized seven thousand Pueblo Indians, prompting King Philip of Spain to declare New Mexico a "royal colony" to be supported by the Crown for the purposes of converting the natives. Santa Fe (literally, "holy faith") was formally established in 1610 as the third and final capital of New Mexico (Oñate had moved his headquarters across the river to the Pueblo of San Gabriel in 1599), and construction began on the Palace of the Governors, the oldest public building in the United States.

A colcha embroidery of the Santo Niño de Atocha by Kathleen Sais Lerner. Many miraculous cures were attributed to the Holy Child by the end of the nineteenth century in New Mexico. Stories abound of his leaving the chapel at night to wander through the countryside, curing the sick, especially children, and in so doing, wearing out his shoes. A common practice that prevails today among the faithful is to make an offering of baby shoes for the Santo Niño to wear on his nightly sojourns.

Oñate returned to Mexico in 1610 and eleven years later journeyed to Spain, the country whose crown he had served but never seen, to clear his name of charges made against him during his tenure in New Mexico. In 1626, he died in Cartagena, Colombia, inspecting a mine on behalf of the Spanish government. Though Oñate never returned to New Mexico after his grand *entrada* of 1598, he left a legacy summed up by his biographer Marc Simmons:

> He was the godfather of the Franciscan missionary program on the northern frontier...He can be credited with launching the livestock industry in the Southwest, for the herds of horses and cattle and flocks of sheep he brought in 1598 furnished a foundation for ranching. He inaugurated mining and the first processing of ores. And he made a notable contribution, through his wide-ranging explorations, toward an understanding of the true geography of western America.

> Oñate's grandest achievement, of course, resided in his establishment of a new kingdom . . . within the Spanish empire . . . . That realm of which he was the architect, while not evolving into the viceroyalty he had hoped, did grow to become the chief anchor and most populous province in the Spanish Borderlands.

> By now it also appears fairly certain that Oñate deserves partial and perhaps even primary honors for the founding of Santa Fe, which exists today as one of the oldest cities in America and the first surviving municipality erected in the West. His accolades, moreover, include the designation of roadblazer, since he was the man who opened and marked the Camino Real from the Chihuahuan mining settlements to northern New Mexico. That was the first established thoroughfare laid out by Europeans within a portion of the present limits of the United States.

Oñate unfortunately also left a legacy of hatred and distrust among the Pueblo Indians. In 1599, he exacted swift retribution on the Acoma Indians, who had killed his nephew and a number of Spanish soldiers in two rebellions, by ordering that each male over the age of twenty-five have his right foot cut off and be sentenced to twenty years of servitude. He also sentenced all other males between ages twelve and twenty-five and all females over age twelve to twenty years of enforced service, though most managed to escape their owners within two years, returning to Acoma to rebuild their village. If Oñate's vengeance was ruthless, he felt it was equal to the treachery of the Acoma, who had hurled Spanish soldiers to their deaths from the pinnacle of their four-hundred-foot "Sky City." In 1614, Oñate stood trial in Mexico for this and other crimes charged against him by members of his expedition. Ironically, as part of his punishment the court ordered that Oñate be permanently banished from New Mexico, a sentence he would spend the rest of his days trying to revoke.

During the seventeenth century, tensions mounted between the Spanish and the Pueblo Indians. The fledgling economy of New Mexico was based on the *encomienda* system established by the Spanish Crown, which permitted appointed members of the colonial aristocracy and the church to "oversee" groups of Pueblo Indians from whom they collected annual tributes of blankets and food. In return the Spanish provided religious education with an eye to converting the Pueblo peoples and offered them protection from attacks by nomadic tribes. Though trade routes

The Mission at San Felipe Pueblo, 1899.

had become firmly established along the Camino Real between New Spain and New Mexico, supply caravans for the missions and settlers only came to the territory every three years, and the colonizers depended upon tributes from the Indians for their own survival.

But even more grating to the Pueblo tribes was the religious fervor with which the Franciscan missionaries approached their charge of proselytizing, systematically destroying *kivas* (ceremonial chambers) and sacred objects, banning the practice of native religions, and persecuting Pueblo religious leaders. The Indians were also forced to build many of the Spanish missions at the various pueblos and to work the Spaniards' fields rather than their own during planting and harvest seasons, jeopardizing their own crops and food supplies (see page 17).

All of this would have been sufficient provocation for the Pueblo Revolt, but in 1666 a major drought hit the Southwest and lasted for five years, drastically depleting the harvest for those years and causing widespread starvation among the already demoralized Pueblo Indians. In 1680, in a singular act of unity, the Pueblo people rose up against the Spanish, killing missionaries and civilians alike, destroying as many churches as they could and driving the remaining survivors out of New Mexico south to El Paso. It was the most successful Indian rebellion ever staged within the boundaries of the United States. For twelve years, the Pueblo tribes kept the Spanish outside New Mexico, but in 1692–93, the newly appointed governor of New Mexico, Captain General Diego de Vargas Zapata Luján Ponce de León y Contreras, successfully led the reconquest of New Mexico, escorting the settlers back into the frontier territory, much as Oñate had done almost one hundred years earlier.

If the seventeenth-century colonization of New Mexico was characterized by political turmoil and conflict between two converging cultures, the eighteenth century ushered in a period of relative economic stability and tolerance between the Pueblo tribes and the Spanish. Chastened by the devastating effects of the Pueblo Revolt, the Spanish Crown rescinded the encomienda system, protecting the rights of the Indians with specific land grants. The Pueblos were allowed to practice their native religions, although many embraced Catholicism. New churches were founded to replace the missions destroyed during the revolt: San José de Laguna at Laguna Pueblo in 1699, the Chapel of San

Miguel in Santa Fe in 1710, Santa Cruz de la Cañada in 1733, and so on. The Spanish and Pueblo peoples offered each other protection against raids by Comanches, Navajos, Utes, and Apaches. And New Mexico began to develop its own unique character, separate from Mexico and Spain, that would express itself in a flourishing art tradition.

Spanish imperialism affected not only the Pueblo tribes but the Spanish colonists as well, who, unlike their titled leaders, would not return to Mexico or Spain to increase their personal wealth and rank among the nobility by their achievements on the new frontier. Rather, they were set adrift in a wilderness, isolated by thousands of miles from one mother country and by an ocean from another, to become citizens of a brand new world. As they pushed further into northern New Mexico during the eighteenth century to found their villages and establish an economy based on farming and sheep herding, the colonists also became isolated from the local seats of power at Santa Fe and Albuquerque (founded in 1706), and, ironically, from the church itself. The Franciscan missionaries, mandated to Christianize New Mexico, concentrated on converting the Pueblo Indians to Catholicism rather than ministering to the settlers themselves. In addition, the vast expanse of the New Mexico territory spread the work of the few priests even thinner.

This isolation from the centers of culture and commerce spurred the Spanish Colonial pioneers to look to their own faith and resources to carve out a meaningful and creative existence in a rugged and harsh environment. Separated from Mexico by great distances and from the rest of the United States until the opening of the Santa Fe Trail in 1821, it became imperative that local villages produce their own goods, which in turn evolved into the unique art forms indigenous to New Mexico.

Prior to the Pueblo Revolt of 1680, Hispanic settlers depended upon imports from Mexico, producing only a limited number of items themselves, notably textiles and furniture. Workshops (*obrajes*) for weaving were established in New Mexico by the 1630s, using both American Indian and Hispanic weavers to produce commercial textiles for export to New Spain. The Pueblo tribes, who had a long tradition of weaving cotton on vertical looms, were a ready source of labor and quickly adapted to the Spanish treadle loom.

A bulto of Nuestra Señora del Carmen by nineteenth-century santero José Rafael Aragón.

Native Americans also proved to be skilled furniture makers under the tutelage of Spanish *carpinteros*. One carpenter had been part of Oñate's expedition into New Mexico. That single number multiplied to forty by the end of the eighteenth century and was, perhaps, even higher, as New Mexicans had to provide almost everything for themselves: chests for storage, chairs, shelved wall cupboards, tables, and armoires, which they decorated with carved designs in relief, or painted. Using native ponderosa pine, Hispanic furniture makers also made doors and altars for their churches in simple, clean lines.

Alcario Otero's *Angel de la Navidad* (Christmas angel) is constructed with a "hollow frame," where the shape of the dress is formed by gessoed cloth draped over a frame and then painted. This technique was practiced by the historic santeros.

After the reconquest of New Mexico under de Vargas, settlers and missionaries spread out north and south of Santa Fe, establishing towns and building churches up and down the Rio Grande. The new churches needed altar pieces and images of saints, as did villagers for their private devotions at home, and local artisans began to fill the needs of church officials and villagers alike. By the middle of the eighteenth century, New Mexico's era of *santero* art had begun.

A *santero* is an image maker, who paints *santos* (saints) on *retablos* (paintings on flat tablets of pine), or carves *bultos* (sculptures) of santos, generally out of cottonwood or aspen. A *reredos* is an altar screen composed of panels of individual santos. From approximately 1750 until the middle of the 1800s, New Mexico experienced a "golden age" of santero art. Artists worked individually and in *talleres,* or workshops, similar to Spanish guilds. For traditional imagery, santeros relied on a few prayer books and mass cards and some religious paintings, all brought from Mexico, which were in turn reflections of European painting styles of the period. By the middle of the nineteenth century, the New Mexican santero had developed his own unique sensibility because of the vacuum in which he worked. It took supply caravans, for example, three years to make the round trip to Mexico and back to New Mexico. When they did arrive, they were primarily carrying items other than religious images, of necessity. With few models to emulate, the New Mexican santero developed his own interpretation of the santos and their lives.

The eighteenth century also saw the expansion of sheep raising, particularly in the Rio Abajo region south of Albuquerque. Most textiles produced in New Mexico in the 1700s were functional, including *jergas* (a multi-use fabric for floor coverings, clothing, and packing material), *sabanillas* (sheeting made of wool), and *frazadas* (blankets). The nineteenth century, however, saw the flowering of Rio Grande weaving under the tutelage of master weavers sent from Mexico to improve the level of that craft in the Rio Arriba area north of Santa Fe. By 1840, more than twenty thousand Rio Grande weavings were exported to Mexico, according to trade manifestos of the day.

Straw appliquéd candle sconces by Félix López.

In 1821, Mexico won its independence from Spain and opened up the Santa Fe Trail to increased trade with the rest of the United States. New goods were suddenly available on the remote frontier. Expanded trade ultimately had an impact on New Mexico's santero arts by the end of the nineteenth century, because mass-produced prayer cards and plaster-cast statues were easily obtained and deemed preferable by the church over the individually painted and carved santos.

Jean Baptiste Lamy, a French-born priest who had immigrated to America, was appointed the first bishop of New Mexico and arrived in Santa Fe in 1851. Under pressure from the increasing number of Protestant sects moving into the territory, Lamy set about strengthening the Catholic church in New Mexico by rebuilding village churches that had fallen into disrepair. He also primarily recruited French-born priests, who preferred to teach their congregations the attributes of the saints through European printed lithographs as opposed to New Mexican handmade retablos. Ironically, these prints stimulated the production of tinwork because they required frames, which tinsmiths provided.

Tinwork began to flourish as a craft after 1846, when tin became more readily available in the form of discarded five-gallon containers used by American army troops in the region. Glass and wallpaper also came over the Santa Fe trail, and soon craftsmen were incorporating these materials into tin frames for religious prints, *nichos* (cabinets) for saints, and boxes for altars and homes. Candle sconces were also popular and necessary for interior lighting, causing tinwork to expand further during the second half of the nineteenth century.

In the eighteenth and nineteenth centuries, Hispanic artisans had also developed the art of straw appliqué to decorate their handmade chests, crosses, boxes, candlesticks, frames, and nichos. Thin slivers of flattened corn husks and wheat straw were cut and applied in a mosaic technique to wooden surfaces prepared with pine pitch. The contrast of the decorative "gold" floral and geometric patterns to their darker wood bases rendered the most commonplace of objects artistic and, in some cases, approximated the gilded extravagance of Spanish and Mexican baroque art.

Furniture, textiles, religious art, tinwork, straw appliqué—these are the crafts the Hispanic colonists transformed into art over a period of two hundred and fifty years before becoming a territory of the United States in 1846. Self-sufficient and determined, they created works of art to adorn their homes and lift their spirits. By the end of the nineteenth century, the Industrial Revolution and the railroad would have a tremendous effect on these art forms, however, as machine-made products and the dollar replaced handmade crafts and the barter system, driving the village economy into decline. Villagers were forced to seek employment away from their hamlets, leading to further decline of their crafts. They worked as laborers on the railroad, as miners, ranch hands and herders, able to return home only on special occasions. While a few continued to make some art for domestic and ecclesiastical use, it would not be until the second decade of the twentieth century that national recognition would focus once again on the Spanish art traditions of New Mexico.

Within the twentieth century, there have been several "cycles of appreciation" of Hispanic art. The first took place at the initiative of a small group of Santa Fe art patrons led by writer Mary Austin and artist Frank Applegate. They traveled often from Santa Fe to the small village of Córdova, especially for the Easter ceremonies. In the course of their visits, they became enamored of the wood carving of José Dolores López and quickly took up the cause of introducing his work to a larger audience and reviving the arts handed down from the Colonial period. The result was the formation in 1925 of the Spanish Colonial Arts Society, whose goals were similar to those of the Society for the Preservation of Spanish Antiquities in New Mexico, which had been founded more than a decade earlier. Both wanted to preserve the traditional arts produced by colonists under Spain (1598–1821) and Mexico (1821–1846) and encourage Hispanic artists to perpetuate those crafts. The Spanish Colonial Arts Society formally incorporated in 1929, the same year it purchased the Santuario de Chimayó from Bernardo Abeyta's descendants. The society's first Spanish Market was held in 1926 and grew each year until

A chip-carved bulto by José Dolores López.

1934, when Mary Austin died—Frank Applegate had died in 1931—and the society became dormant for a number of years.

Ironically, a second cycle of appreciation of Hispanic art took place during the depression of the 1930s, when many villagers lost employment in the outside world and returned home to their small towns. While the Spanish Colonial Arts Society had been formed for artistic and cultural reasons, there was now an economic motivation for a crafts revival that would provide employment to rural Hispanics. This took the form of crafts programs organized by the New Mexico State Department of Vocational Education in 1933. Part of the Federal Art Project of the Works Progress Administration (WPA), these programs were established in virtually every Spanish community in New Mexico by 1936. Many of the pieces of furniture in Santa Fe museums and public buildings, for example, were made during the WPA period. However, World War II intervened, and returning veterans were forced once again to seek employment outside their villages, causing the crafts to recede into the background.

The legacy of José Dolores López is evident in these three bultos. Eurgencio López covers Our Lady of Light (center) with ornate filigree designs, depicting a half moon on the bottom, the symbol of the Virgin, above which he has carved an angel, the Virgin's sash, and rosettes. The individual rays of the crown are also intricately chip-carved. St. Peter by George López (left) is a more somber figure with fewer embellishments on his robe. His attributes are the key he holds to the Kingdom of Heaven and the Bible through which he proclaims Christ's message. José Mondragón's approach is even more minimalist in his San José (right), for which the surface design is spare but elegant, and the emphasis is on the strong shape of the saint.

In 1952, E. Boyd, the renowned curator of Spanish Colonial art for the Museum of New Mexico, resurrected the inactive Spanish Colonial Arts Society, initially to raise funds to collect historic pieces and keep them from leaving the state and, later in 1965, to revive a Spanish Market to stimulate the arts by giving craftspeople a place to sell their work. Since 1967, Spanish Market has been an annual event in Santa Fe, attracting hundreds of artists and thousands of visitors.

This third "revival" in Hispanic art that began in the 1960s and has exploded in the 1990s is the subject of *Across Frontiers*. Proud of their heritage and deeply devoted to their culture and religion, contemporary Hispanic artists have gone beyond the functional craft of their ancestors to create art forms that are fresh and contemporary; at the same time, they are unmistakably rooted in four hundred years of history.

§

Across Frontiers is about the rich diversity of late-twentieth-century Hispanic art and the traditions from which that art has evolved. Most of the artists have developed their careers within the last three decades, although some earlier masters of the twentieth century are included. I have not attempted to write a complete history of the art forms; rather, I have presented a summary of pertinent background information that places the contemporary works in context. Some artists have been selected because they are inaugurating new "traditions" of their own; others exemplify the best of existing traditions. Many have won prestigious awards at Spanish Market; others have never entered Spanish Market. The majority have learned their art from family members and from each other; a few are completely self-taught. All are committed to perpetuating the art forms handed down to them by their Spanish and Mexican forebears.

Chapter 1

Hispanic Weaving
of the
Rio Grande

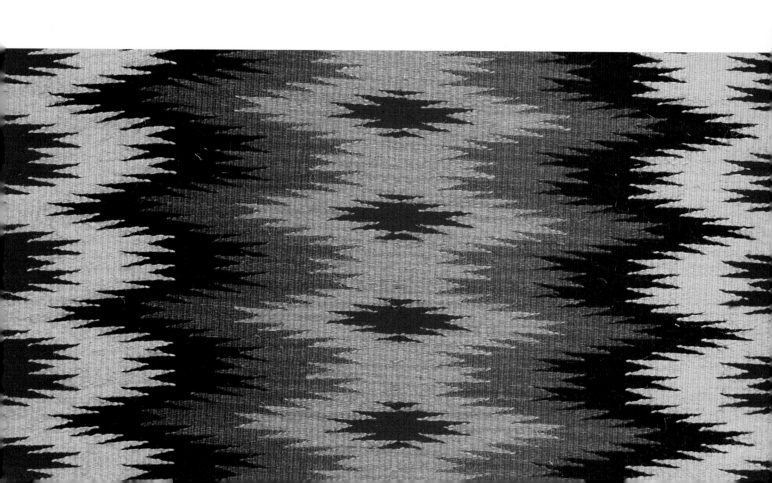

Nicacio Ortega, who founded Ortega's Weaving Shop in Chimayó in 1900, at age eighty-three.

Chimayó with the badlands in the background, 1911. The name Chimayó comes from a nearby hill called Tsi Mayóh by the Tewa Indians. Chimayó has been a center for Spanish weaving since the eighteenth century.

N 1900, Nicacio Ortega founded Ortega's Weaving Shop in Chimayó, New Mexico, launching one of the first commercially successful ventures in Rio Grande textiles headed by a weaver. A fifth-generation weaver, Nicacio was born in 1875, five years before the railroad reached New Mexico in 1880, carrying the first wave of tourists from the East to view what remained of the American frontier. Grabiel Ortega, an ancestor of Nicacio's, had settled in Chimayó in 1758 and is credited by the Ortegas for initiating the craft of weaving in their family. A textile industry based on indigenous labor had been in place before the 1680 Pueblo Revolt in the northern villages and was revived after the reconquest among Spanish men, who passed the craft along to their sons.

Along the route of the Santa Fe Railroad were the famous Harvey Houses, built by the Fred Harvey Company at the end of the nineteenth century, to provide passengers with decent food, good accommodations, and an opportunity to buy genuine handcrafted art by American Indians. The railroad cut through some reservations and passed near others, providing Native Americans with a ready outlet for their crafts among the tourists, who were thrilled to take home souvenirs of the romantic Southwest. Capitalizing on America's fascination with the West, the Fred Harvey Company and the Santa Fe Railroad promoted American Indian cultures in their advertising, creating a national interest in Native American art that would overshadow Hispanic art for several decades.

David Ortega wove this wedding blanket in 1996 for his grandson's wedding. He began weaving in 1931 at age fourteen. In 1948, he and his brother José Ramón built the Ortega Weaving Shop in its current location.

Page 26

In *La Jornada del Mariposa*, Don Leon Sandoval reproduces the brilliant colors of the butterfly's wings in natural dyes.

Page 27, top

In *Northern Lights*, Norma Medina incorporates a Chimayó chevron design within a Saltillo diamond. Using only natural dyes from plants she gathers herself, Medina dyes her wool in the summer months. The blue in this weaving is indigo.

Page 27, bottom

Agueda Martínez wove this large rag rug (82 by 52 inches) from hundreds of different fragments of material. Rag rugs illustrate the Hispanic villager's philosophy that nothing should be wasted.

Built in the California Mission style with a red-tiled roof and arches, the Alvarado Hotel provided one of the earliest retail outlets for Hispanic art along the Santa Fe Railroad. The Santa Fe Railroad also promoted the Southwest and its Indian and Hispanic cultures by sponsoring artists to travel to the West and paint its scenes and subjects.

Traders and dealers in Santa Fe, however, saw an opportunity to incorporate Hispanic textiles into the burgeoning marketplace for Southwest "exotica" by working with Chimayó weavers to create commercial blankets and rugs that appeared "Indian" and would be of an appropriate size for tourists to take home. Design motifs included thunderbirds, arrows, and the four directions—styles that directly rivaled Navajo blankets of the period. In his informative book on Chimayó, *Sabino's Map,* Don Usner notes that the Fred Harvey Company was first to apply the label "Chimayó" to Spanish weavings, leaving the distinction between Indian and Hispanic weavings deliberately vague so that tourists might assume they were Indian-made. Some weavings were promoted as "Chimayó Indian" weavings. In 1902, the Fred Harvey Company opened the Alvarado Hotel in Albuquerque with an adjoining Indian and Mexican Museum Building. This and other retail outlets across the country provided a market for Chimayó weavings.

In describing the beginning of Ortega's Weaving Shop, David Ortega recalls that the Harvey Houses were among the best accounts his father had in the early decades of the twentieth century. To meet the demand for weavings, Nicacio Ortega contracted individuals to fill the

Tierra Wools Panorama, Los Ojos

The demise of the land grant system at the end of the nineteenth century had an impact on the weaving industry in New Mexico by limiting the land available for grazing sheep. In 1983, activist María Varela and rancher Antonio Manzanares founded Ganados del Valle (Livestock in the valley) to revitalize the Chama Valley's sheep ranching and wool industries. They introduced cooperative marketing strategies to Hispanic ranchers, as they fought to restore communal grazing lands established under the land grant system. A churro sheep breeding project was also launched to reclaim the prized churro wool for weavers in the area.

In tandem with the sheep project, Tierra Wools, a weaving cooperative, was started to provide employment for the valley's women. Rachel Brown, a professional weaver and author from Taos, was enlisted to teach local artisans how to spin wool on the spinning wheel rather than with the traditional hand spindle, or *malacate*. With Brown's help, weavers also built sturdier looms, replaced cotton with wool warps, learned updated dyeing methods, and found a home in a one-hundred-year-old mercantile building on the only street in Los Ojos.

Every weaver in Tierra Wools participates in all aspects of the business, including production management, sales, and marketing. Some weavers work at home; others schedule time on the multiple looms in the back room of Tierra Wools. All dyeing is done on the premises, and visitors can observe weavers at work and watch spinning demonstrations.

Tierra Wools weavers Johanna Terrazas, Mary Velasquez, Sophie Martínez, and Nena Russom wove the pieces in this collage.

Jacobo O. "Jake" Trujillo wove this richly detailed weaving to teach his son, Irvin, all of the classic Chimayó designs: chevrons, diamonds, hourglass motifs, and leaves (also called *manitas,* or little hands), which are outlined by either step designs or serrated edges.

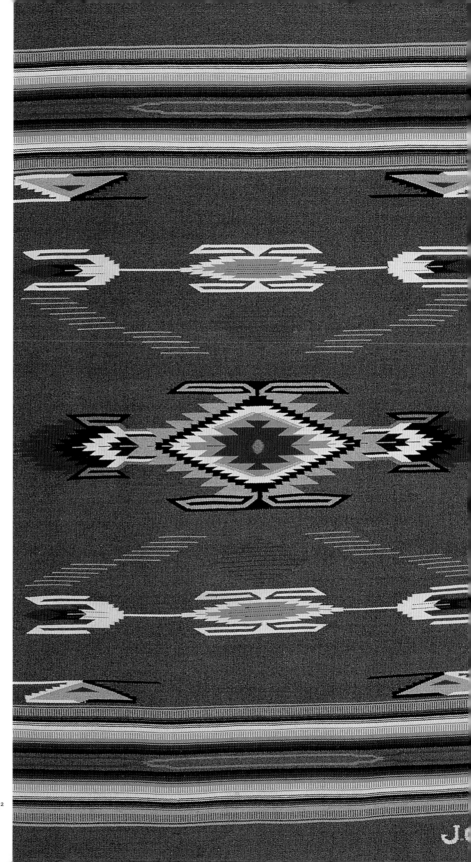

orders he couldn't complete himself, providing them with wool, yarn, and designs. Today, Ortega's Weaving Shop employs four full-time weavers and fifty additional contract weavers from Cundiyo, Truchas, Medanales, Española, and other northern New Mexican villages to make the rugs, vests, placemats, pillows, coats, and art weavings they sell directly to the public. Contract weaving is a way of life in Chimayó. Centinela Traditional Arts, owned and operated by Irvin and Lisa Trujillo, employs approximately ten contract weavers, as does John Trujillo, a relative and owner of Trujillo's Weaving Shop. In several families, everyone weaves—father, mother, and children—and it is not unusual to visit a home in Chimayó and find a loom in every room.

The "Chimayó" style has a central pattern, usually a diamond or chevron motif, which is bordered on either end by horizontal bands. A repeating design motif often flanks the central form. Abstract versions of the thunderbird are popular variations. Both synthetic and natural vegetal dyes are used today, producing designs in a wide range of colors. The wedding blanket by David Ortega features a central diamond with a step design bordered by two lighter chevron designs, which are further framed by smaller versions of the central pattern (see page 29).

While the Chimayó weaving may have evolved in response to the tourist era of the railroad (1880–1920), it incorporates patterns that are classic to Hispanic weaving, derived from Rio Grande and Saltillo textiles that reached their zenith in the sixty years preceding the railroad. The basic Rio Grande blanket consists of alternating wide horizontal bands with narrow panels of stripes. Early Rio Grande blankets were composed of odd-numbered bands, such as five-band or seven-band patterns, between which were narrow panels (see page 2). The weavings are longer than they are wide, and are generally woven in two panels on a narrow treadle loom and stitched together in the middle. Rio Grande blankets, used as wearing blankets during the day and for bedding at night, were produced in New Mexico for three centuries for personal use among the Spanish colonists, for trade with Native Americans, and for export to Mexico.

Jacobo O. "Jake" Trujillo (1911–1990)

Jake Trujillo's life typifies the experience of many Hispanic weavers unable to devote themselves full-time to weaving because they had to seek employment outside their villages. Like many men of his generation, Trujillo learned to weave as a young boy in Chimayó and built his own loom when he was sixteen. He worked for an uncle who was a dealer, and he taught weaving, dyeing, and spinning in vocational programs during the WPA era. After World War II, though, Trujillo and his wife moved to Los Alamos because of employment opportunities and schooling for their children. Jake returned to Chimayó on weekends, where he continued to weave. He did not take up weaving full-time, however, until his retirement in 1975, when he returned to Chimayó. In 1982, Jake and his family founded Centinela Traditional Arts at their ranch of the same name just outside Chimayó. Weavers like Trujillo sustained the tradition of Hispanic weaving, even when it could not sustain them.

A weaver in Chimayó, ca. 1917. Though cumbersome in appearance, the treadle loom is ideally suited for commercial textile production because one can weave yardage of any length or individual pieces without having to warp the loom each time.

To produce weavings, the Spanish established *obrajes,* or workshops, based loosely on the European guild system in which the arts were organized by task, and individuals became skilled masters in specific areas. For weaving, the division of labor included carding, spinning, dyeing, weaving, and warping the loom. The Spanish treadle loom made production work easier, because it was designed to store extensive lengths of warp on a horizontal warp beam. The warp is the foundation of a weaving and consists of parallel threads that are held in tension by the front and back beam, around which the weft, or filler threads, are woven to create the weaving. The treadles, or foot pedals, operate the heddle shafts, or harnesses, which are a system of pulleys, separating individual warp threads from each other.

When the Spanish colonized New Mexico under Oñate in 1598, they encountered a skilled labor force in the Pueblo Indian tribes, who already had a sophisticated weaving tradition of their own. The Pueblo weavers used a vertical loom to weave cotton cloth for clothing, belts, and *mantas,* or blankets, which could be either worn or used for bedding. Unlike the Spanish *sarape,* the Pueblo manta is wider than it is long. In both Spanish and Pueblo cultures during the Spanish Colonial period, men were the primary weavers, while women became the weavers among the Navajo.

Teresa Archuleta-Sagel embroiders colcha at her home in Española

A renowned weaver whose work has been collected by nine museums, including the Smithsonian's National Museum of American History, Teresa Archuleta-Sagel is also a noted scholar of Rio Grande weaving. She wrote the informative introduction on contemporary weaving for *Rio Grande Textiles* (1994) and has most recently written the historical chapter on Spanish textiles for *Spanish New Mexico* (1996), among many publications. A poet as well, Archuleta-Sagel often bases her contemporary weavings on her poems. She is also well known for her scholarship on colcha and for bringing back the wool sabanilla foundation for colcha the historic weavers used. Like her teacher and mentor, Agueda Martínez, she has been an instructor in classic and contemporary weaving in workshops across the state, inspiring the next generation of weavers to understand the traditions and techniques behind Rio Grande textiles.

Entitled *Jardín de mis Delicias* (Garden of my Delights), this colcha by Teresa Archuleta-Sagel is embroidered with floral patterns reminiscent of East Indian chintz fabric imported during the Spanish Colonial period.

A classic Saltillo sarape, which would have been made between 1700 and 1850, is distinguished by the fineness of its weave and its design motifs. In this piece, red serrated diamonds within white serrated diamonds compose the intricate background pattern. Within the central diamond and border are distinct designs. This textile was produced ca. 1750–1825.

Weaving was an established export business by the 1630s in New Mexico, according to trade manifestos of the time, employing both Spanish and Native American weavers in the obrajes. The *churro* sheep, brought to the New World by the Spanish, provided wool, and within a short period of time, the Pueblo weavers had incorporated wool into their own weaving tradition. The churro's wool is especially well suited for weaving because its long straight fibers can be handspun into a fine yarn, and its low lanolin content makes it easier to dye than a greasy wool that is difficult to clean.

After the reconquest of New Mexico by de Vargas in 1692–1696, the weaving industry shifted to the region south of Albuquerque. The land grant system, instituted by the Spanish Crown before the Pueblo Revolt, once again enticed colonists to resettle, and the large tracts of land were ideal for sheep ranching. By 1790, one-third of the households in the region listed weaving as their occupation. Sheep were also raised for export to Mexico, which became a thriving business for the colonists in the nineteenth century. In 1835, for example, more than eighty thousand sheep were sold to Mexico.

Weaving in the area north of Santa Fe had declined, however, to the point that New Mexico Governor Fernando Chacón complained in 1802 that the lack of formalized training had compromised the quality of New Mexico's textiles. In response to Chacón's complaints, two master weavers, Juan and Ygnacio Bazán, were sent from Mexico City to Santa Fe in 1807 to improve the quality of weaving in the Rio Arriba area. During the brothers' two-year tenure, they revitalized weaving north of Santa Fe through instruction in design, dyeing, spinning, and weaving. There is some evidence as well that they introduced Rio Grande weavers to the technical intricacies of the exquisite Saltillo sarapes.

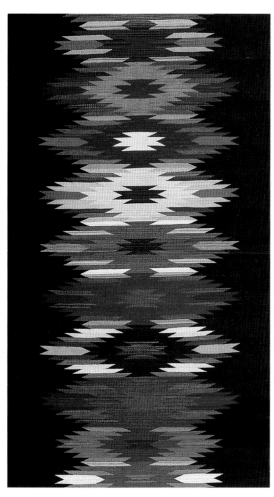

One of the founders of the Tierra Wools weaving cooperative, Johanna Terrazas is noted for her use of black as a background color to contrast with her vivid colors. The contemporary design of this textile entitled *Yesterday* pays tribute to the Saltillo diamond and chevron motifs.

Saltillo is a town in the state of Coahuila in northern Mexico and the site of important trade fairs since the end of the seventeenth century. San Esteban de Tlaxcala is a barrio within Saltillo that was colonized by Tlaxcalan Indians in 1591 at the request of the Spanish government, who had recruited them to pass on their knowledge of farming and the arts to the *Chichamecas,* semi-nomadic Indians, who frequently threatened settlements. The Tlaxcalans had a long and distinguished history of weaving, which they brought with them to Saltillo and which they adapted to the Spanish treadle loom. They developed the Saltillo sarape, which became a prized possession of the Spanish on both sides of the border and a status symbol among wealthy *hacendados* (landowners), who competed with each other for the most intricately patterned Saltillos. Saltillos were also woven in other parts of New Spain, particularly San Miguel de Allende, but the main production center was in Saltillo itself.

Joe Ben Wheat, a noted scholar of textiles, describes the Saltillo pattern in *Rio Grande Textiles* as a "large and very complex central diamond motif composed of concentric serrate bands, with a background of solid color relieved by diagonal rows or a grid of tiny figures....or one composed of vertically oriented serrate figures and a figured border." A circle or medallion sometimes replaces the central diamond. The patterns that comprise the serrated diamond or lozenge may be any of a number of complex designs: hourglass figures, zigzag lines, leaf motifs, double diamonds, and chevrons. Design elements are generally serrated and colors are brilliant. A variety of reds derived from cochineal are used in combination with all the assorted shades of indigo. The Saltillo typically has a border containing more intricate designs that complement the complexity of the center pattern. Woven in two parts and stitched together, the Saltillo may have a slit in the middle for the head so it can be worn over the body like a poncho, with the central diamond framing the upper body.

The Tlaxcalan weavers in Mexico used a very fine cotton warp and handspun their wool to be equally fine, producing three times as many warp and weft counts per inch as the New Mexican weavers were able to do with their thicker wool. The nineteenth-century New Mexican weavings consequently had fewer but larger design patterns and less intricate backgrounds than the Saltillos. Perhaps because it could take a weaver up to eight or nine months of ten-hour days to complete an extremely intricate Saltillo, it may have become economically prohibitive for weavers to continue making the exquisite tapestries. By 1850, the Saltillo had peaked in excellence and production began to wane thereafter. The legacy of the Tlaxcalans' weaving genius, however, would be felt throughout the nineteenth and twentieth centuries, as the Rio Grande weavers began incorporating design elements from Saltillo sarapes into their own blankets, culminating in the fine work of contemporary Hispanic weavers.

The opening of the Santa Fe Trail in 1821 created new markets for New Mexican textiles. Most obrajes of the period continued to produce commercial yardage in the form of *jerga,* a thick plaid or striped twill weave used for floor coverings, as well as for clothing and yardage for packing; *frazadas* (long blankets); and *sabanilla,* a handspun wool sheeting used for some clothing, mattress ticks, and the backing for *colcha* embroidery. This type of embroidery typically uses vegetal-dyed handspun wool yarn on wool sabanilla; it evolved in colonial New Mexico. *Colcha* means "quilt" or "bedspread" in Spanish, although, as E. Boyd points out in *Popular Arts of Spanish New Mexico,* "the New Mexican colcha is not a quilt in the sense of being a cover filled with inner material and tacked or quilted to hold the contents in place. Such a quilt in New Mexico is called a colchón. The regional colcha was first a hanging which was solidly embroidered with wool yarns so that none of its woolen support was visible." Church records indicate that colcha altar cloths were in use by the eighteenth century in New Mexico. Colchas were also used as bed coverings and decorative textiles.

Rio Saltillo by Teresa Archuleta-Sagel is based upon a nineteenth-century Rio Grande blanket composed of Saltillo sarape designs and layout: a central serrated diamond motif surrounded by a field of smaller repeating bicolored diamonds, side borders, and striped borders on either end.

Blue Colonia by Delores Medina Archuleta combines traditional Rio Grande horizontal bands with Saltillo designs in various shades of indigo blue and natural wools. *Colonia* refers to the Spanish Colonial period of weaving, in which indigo blue dominated the palette of weavers.

A wool-on-wool colcha by María Vergara-Wilson is embroidered with handspun wool dyed with Spanish Colonial dyes: indigo, cochineal, cota, chamisa, brazilwood, and walnut hulls. She also wove the sabanilla foundation. The floral design is inspired by East Indian cotton chintz patterns.

Patterns for the wool-on-wool embroideries include elaborate floral designs derived from silk shawls and fabric traded into Mexico and New Mexico from India and the Far East in the Colonial period. In place of lightweight linen and silk threads, New Mexican women used thicker wool yarns to embroider the soft wool sabanilla in a self-couching stitch—one long stitch caught in the middle by a shorter diagonal stitch—creating their own distinctive art form.

Trade routes into New Mexico were further expanded when the United States won the Southwest territories from Mexico in the 1848 Treaty of Guadalupe Hidalgo. Commercial supplies poured into New Mexico, including manufactured cotton cloth, woolen yarns, and ready-made clothing. The increasing availability of cotton gradually led to wool-on-cotton colchas and a diminishing use of sabanilla. By the end of the nineteenth century, the availability of inexpensive manufactured cloth and clothing would make a serious dent in the Spanish textile export business, turning weavers toward a commercial tourist market.

Prior to the 1850s, indigo dominated the palette in Hispanic weaving, providing shades from the deepest to the palest blue. The Spanish imported indigo dye from Mexico in the seventeenth century, and the early blankets of Spanish, Pueblo, and Navajo weavers consisted of banded patterns of alternating natural brown and white wool with indigo blue. This pattern was called "the Mexican Pelt" by Navajo weavers, reflecting the influence of the Spanish upon indigenous weaving. Indigo also combined with the local New Mexican *chamisa,* or rabbit brush, to produce green. Chamisa in turn furnished a wide range of yellows and ochres. For a variety of reds, cochineal was imported from Mexico and Central America. An expensive dye, cochineal is made from the dried bodies of the female cochineal insect that feeds on the prickly pear cactus. So difficult to harvest was cochineal that it became second only to silver in export value in sixteenth-century New Spain. Brazilwood, another source for differing shades of red and terra-cotta, was also imported from Mexico; some brazilwood reds eventually faded to tans and ochres. Black walnut hulls, onion skins, and juniper bark yielded various shades of brown; *cota,* also called Navajo tea, produced a rich variety of ambers and rusts.

The eight-pointed star motif, which defines the Vallero style, is tightly woven with Germantown yarn in this nineteenth-century Rio Grande textile.

The first synthetic dyes, discovered in 1856, had a tremendous impact on Hispanic and Native American designs, introducing a seemingly unlimited range of brilliant new colors. Aniline dyes both expanded the weaver's artistic possibilities and made the dyeing process infinitely easier. Dyeing under any circumstances requires multiple steps of washing and rinsing to clean the wool and remove debris from the fibers. Without a mordant, wool won't "hold" the dye. Before the advent of synthetic dyes, alum was used to *mordant* the wool, as was fermented urine, the only substance that would dissolve indigo.

Germantown, Pennsylvania, was the manufacturing hub of commercially dyed yarn in the 1860s, much of which was distributed to Navajo weavers. Hispanic weavers also used Germantown yarn, initially for small design elements in their textiles and later for entire weavings that exploded in color. The even quality of the yarn, in contrast to handspun yarn, produced tightly woven pieces that are examples of technical virtuosity, such as the Germantown *Vallero*.

Characterized by vivid colors, detailed vertical borders, and multiple eight-pointed stars, the Vallero appears to be a first cousin of the earlier Saltillo. The central motif of a star recalls the diamond or lozenge of the Saltillo, while the background figures and the main pattern are outlined with serrated edges. Popularized by the Montoya sisters, who lived in El Valle in the late nineteenth century, the weavings became known as Valleros. The stars in the Vallero have been attributed to American quilt patterns or stars in the American flag. The pattern may also have roots in Moorish Spain and would have been imported to the New World through Spanish colonization. Teresa Archuleta-Sagel, a contemporary weaver, notes that the eight-pointed star is similar to the "Spanish

Wheel" design popular among Moslem weavers, who worked in Spanish obrajes. Whatever its origin, the Vallero marks the end of nineteenth-century Rio Grande weaving and reflects the natural ingenuity of Hispanic weavers to adapt motifs from their changing world into their textiles.

Commercial textile production for export began to wane in the last quarter of the nineteenth century, because the weavers could not compete economically with the mass-produced textiles coming into New Mexico via the railroad. In addition, the *merino* sheep had been introduced to New Mexico in 1859. The high lanolin content of the merino's wool made it extremely difficult to clean and dye evenly. Cross-breeding of the churro with the merino and *rambouillet* sheep, another breed raised for meat production, eventually contaminated the churro to the point that the wool was no longer as ideally suited for weaving as it had once been.

For three centuries, Spanish textiles were produced in New Mexico for export and domestic use. Besides providing the essentials for themselves—blankets, floor coverings, and woolen sarapes to protect against the bitter New Mexican winters—colonists developed a thriving textile business that contributed substantially to New Mexico's economy during its years under Spain (1598–1821) and Mexico (1821–1846). Under the United States occupation beginning in 1846, New Mexico's weaving industry gradually shifted from an export market to production geared to the new tourism spurred by railroad travel to the West.

During the transitional period in weaving from 1880 to 1920, a home-based cottage industry of contract labor replaced the obraje system of organized production. With a changing market also came a changing aesthetic, as traders encouraged weavers to create designs that would appeal to the tourist. Much as Lorenzo Hubbell had transformed Navajo weaving at the end of the nineteenth century from striped blankets to oriental-patterned rugs to appeal to collectors of the eastern United States, so too did traders promote the transformation of New Mexico's Hispanic weaving from Rio Grande blankets to Chimayó rugs.

§

The Falling Stars by Karen Martínez includes Vallero, Saltillo, and Rio Grande designs. The lightning pattern on the side panels was particularly popular in nineteenth-century textiles.

A classic Saltillo-style weaving by Lisa Trujillo. Alternating serrated diamonds and leaf patterns compose the zigzag lines of the background.

In the twentieth century, Hispanic weaving of the Rio Grande has evolved into a highly creative art form through both patronage and a renewed interest among weavers in their historic roots. Teresa Archuleta-Sagel sums up the experience of many contemporary weavers:

We awoke to our own heritage through a desire to create art that reflected our own cultural identity. Our work was an act of self-discovery that stirred intense feelings of pride and self-worth, and the style and tradition in which we worked provided the means to connect with and, in some cases, re-create roots that needed our vigor and vision. We became as midwives attending our community and helping to ensure that it would survive the twentieth century and, indeed, flower into the twenty-first century.

A scholar of Rio Grande weaving, Archuleta-Sagel attributes much of the current interest in historic weaving to the 1979 publication of *Spanish Textile Tradition of New Mexico and Colorado* by the Museum of New Mexico Press (reissued with new material in 1994 as *Rio Grande Textiles*). In 1976 and 1979, the Museum of International Folk Art in Santa Fe had sponsored workshops in weaving and dyeing, making available for study the museum's extraordinary collection of historic Rio Grande textiles. The 1979 publication was important for Archuleta-Sagel and other weavers because it gave them a "historical context," for the first time, in which to place their own work, inspiring many weavers with a new appreciation and interest in their artistic antecedents.

The Saltillo sarape presents, perhaps, the greatest technical challenge to contemporary weavers because of the intricacy of its repeating designs and colors. *Devotion* by Lisa Trujillo has a classic Saltillo design layout with a central serrated diamond, a serrated vertical background pattern, and repeating motifs in the borders. Contemporary additions are the heart in the center diamond and the colors: in place of the strong reds and blues of Mexican Saltillos, Trujillo combines muted pastels of mauve and rose from cochineal and pale blues from indigo with four natural wool colors.

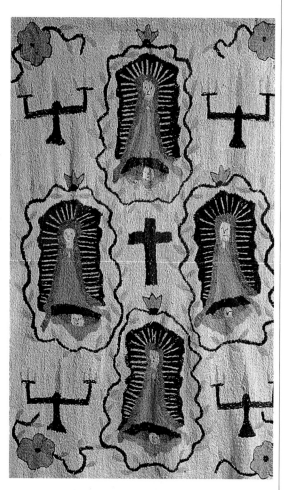

Colcha embroidery undergoes a renaissance in the twentieth century

One of the textile arts that has received renewed interest among contemporary weavers is colcha embroidery. In the twentieth century, colcha has undergone several significant revivals. The first occurred in the 1930s in Carson, New Mexico, a predominantly Mormon community, through the efforts of a trader named Elmer Shupe, who asked his sister-in-law, Frances Varos Graves, to repair an antique wool-on-wool colcha so it could be sold. Graves soon began making her own colchas, inspiring a number of Carson ladies to follow suit, and a small home industry began to flourish. These embroideries, typically made from recycled materials, have a distinctly folk art appeal. This Carson colcha, which measures 6 by 4 feet, portrays angels holding the Virgin of Guadalupe. The lines framing each Guadalupe are adorned with a fleur-de-lis pattern, representing the Trinity, and flowers decorate the corners of the piece. The floating cross and candelabra may allude to the trappings of an altar.

At the same time that the Carson colcha made its appearance, 1930s WPA-sponsored crafts programs were created in outlying rural communities to sustain traditional Spanish crafts, including weaving and colcha embroidery. A goal of these programs was to establish another source of revenue for rural New Mexican villages through cottage industries in the crafts. *The New Mexico Colonial Embroidery Bulletin*, written by Carmen Espinosa in 1935 for the Department of Vocational Education and Training, contained a variety of colcha patterns. Distributed across the state to community programs, it was a guidebook for weavers into the early 1940s.

A third revival in colcha has occurred over the last twenty-five years in response to weavers' interest in their historic antecedents. While the colcha stitch has its counterparts in other cultures, the wool-on-wool colchas of the Spanish Colonial period may be completely indigenous to New Mexico. As such, colcha embroidery has become an emblem of cultural pride among contemporary Hispanic weavers, such as Teresa Archuleta-Sagel and María Vergara-Wilson, who both weave their own wool sabanilla and use handspun and hand-dyed wool for their embroidery. Other artists, such as renowned tinsmith Senaida Romero and her granddaughter Donna Wright de Romero, incorporate colcha embroidery into tin pieces (see chapter 3).

María Fernandez Graves uses both wool and cotton foundations, as well as commercial yarns and recycled wool clothing for her colchas, which reflect the style of her aunt, Frances Varos Graves. The background color for this colcha altar cloth comes from the raveled yarn of a sweater. It is embroidered in the style of the Carson colchas with figures of San Rafael, the Good Shepherd, and the Santo Niño de Atocha on the top row and San Ysidro, Nuestra Señora de Guadalupe, and St. Agnes on the bottom.

Eppie Archuleta embellishes the background of this classic Chimayó weaving with a pattern of dots and dashes and outlines the central diamond of each figure with the Navajo step design. The great-great-granddaughter of a Navajo *criada*, Archuleta is also well known for her *Yei* weavings after the Navajo word for Holy People.

The most popular Saltillo motif used in contemporary Hispanic textiles is the serrated diamond, which has many variations. Eppie Archuleta, for example, adds the step design found on Navajo textiles and Pueblo pottery to the central serrated pattern and the four diamonds that flank it in her classic Chimayó weaving (see page 47). And Agueda Martínez transforms a single diamond motif into a repeating pattern in her brilliantly colored weaving.

Doña Agueda, as Agueda Martínez is known to students and collectors alike, is the matriarch of Hispanic weaving in the Southwest. Born in Chamita in 1898, she learned to make rag rugs as a teenager from an elderly neighbor. Like many women from her generation, though, Doña Agueda developed her weaving skills under the direction of two men from Chimayó: her husband, Eusebio Martínez (whom she married in 1916), and a cousin and godfather of one of her children, Lorenzo Trujillo, who had a trading post in Chimayó. During the first part of the twentieth century, men were still the primary Hispanic weavers, and women performed the tasks of carding, spinning, and dyeing the wool. With the advent of World War II, many men left the villages, and women soon took over all aspects of weaving.

Agueda Martínez wove this Saltillo-style textile at age ninety-eight.

Agueda Martínez at age ninety-eight weaving on her loom in Medanales

Doña Agueda and her husband, Eusebio Martínez, moved to rural Medanales in 1924 (a tiny village of only three hundred and fifty people today), where they farmed during the spring and summer months and turned to weaving during the winter. Weaving provided another source of income besides farming to support their ten children during the harsh years of the depression and World War II, when northern New Mexico's economy plummeted to a record low. Since her husband's death in 1962, Doña Agueda has continued to farm and weave full-time, making Medanales an important center for Hispanic weaving.

Among Doña Agueda's daughters, Eppie Archuleta and Cordelia Coronado have tirelessly promoted traditional Hispanic weaving through countless workshops they have run for hundreds of weavers. In 1988, Archuleta bought and restored the Tres Piedras Mill, which had provided Hispanic weavers with wool since the 1930s.

This is the first piece Teresa Archuleta-Sagel wove after a long illness. "Interestingly enough," she says, "this 'come-back' piece was finished on the feast day of Nuestra Señora de Guadalupe, and quite serendipitously the green and rose colors that I chose to use in the weaving are similar to Guadalupe's colors."

During the more than eighty years she has been weaving, Doña Agueda has taught four generations of her own family to weave—there are more than seventy weavers in her family. She has also taught master weavers like Teresa Archuleta-Sagel, as well as many others, in government-sponsored programs such as HELP (Home Education Livelihood Program), insuring a strong future for the historic Rio Grande style, which has become one of the signature weavings of Doña Agueda's descendants and students. *La Guadalupana* by Teresa Archuleta-Sagel is a classic five-banded Rio Grande pattern with serrated Saltillo chevrons incorporated into each band. The bands themselves are separated by plain horizontal lines of color, divided further by bands featuring half-leaf patterns, for which Archuleta-Sagel is well known.

This traditional band-and-stripe Rio Grande textile by Cordelia Coronado is dyed with indigo blue and incorporates serrated diamonds in the white bands.

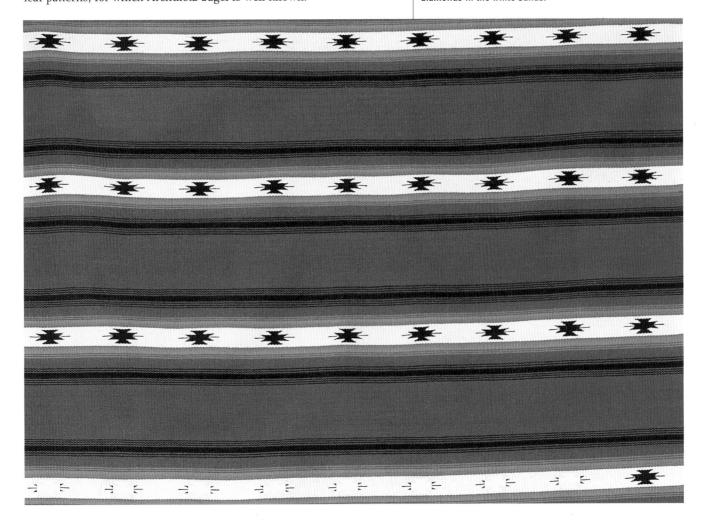

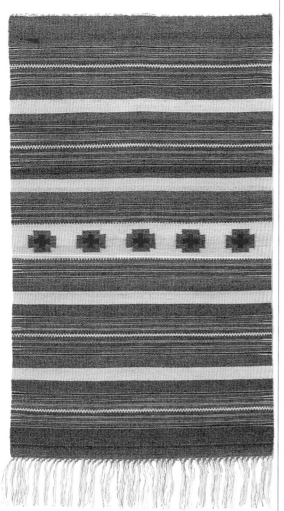

This traditional five-banded Rio Grande weaving by Rita Padilla Haufmann has a cross pattern in the central band. The various shades of rose are derived from cochineal.

The Rio Grande band-and-stripe style is popular among a number of weavers, including Rita Padilla Haufmann, who uses only homespun natural and dyed churro wool in her textiles. Completely self-taught, Haufmann goes through multiple steps to prepare the wool. She buys a whole fleece of churro wool, which is thoroughly washed and rinsed at least four times. After drying overnight, the fleece is carded to eliminate any other debris and to align the fibers for spinning. To card enough wool for a 31-by-50-inch weaving takes approximately four hours. The third step is spinning the wool, after which it is wound into skeins on a niddy noddy, a wooden T-frame apparatus. The skeins are washed and rinsed one more time to remove any remaining dirt; the last rinse contains a few drops of pennyroyal oil, or *poleo,* as a moth repellent. The skeins are then dried under tension overnight. After these steps, the wool is ready for dyeing. Haufmann prepares all of her own dyes from plant material, straining the dye bath to remove debris. She uses alum as a mordant, after which she places the wool in its dye bath in a *solar pot* to bake in the sun for four or five hours, which produces brighter colors.

Don Leon Sandoval is another contemporary weaver who uses churro wool and natural dyes in his weavings, which range from classic Rio Grande band-and-stripe designs to Saltillo "eyedazzlers." In *La Jornada del Mariposa* (see page 26), the aqua green is produced by overdyeing indigo with snakeweed *(yerba de la víbora),* which produces yellow, while the bright green is produced by overdyeing indigo with chamisa. The other colors are from cochineal, indigo, and the churro's natural black wool.

While Saltillo motifs and Rio Grande band-and-stripe designs characterize much of historic and contemporary Hispanic textiles, some weavers are noted for their pictorials. Pictorials require a tapestry weave technique, in which the picture is formed by various colored, discontinuous wefts. (*Tapestry* also refers to the fineness of a weave, made possible by spinning the yarn to a very thin diameter so that the thread counts per inch range between ninety to one hundred and twenty or more.) Norma Medina and Irene López have both chosen religious themes for their pictorials. Medina's weaving entitled *My Strength* frames the Calvary Cross within a Chimayó weaving. The top and bottom borders repeat the horizontal bands and serrated chevrons of the Chimayó, while the side borders alternate two styles of serrated diamonds.

My Strength, a textile by Norma Medina, frames the Calvary Cross within a Chimayó weaving.

Irene López's pictorial of Nuestro Señor de Esquípulas includes natural dyes of indigo, cochineal, cota, and cedar chips. The background color and the body of Christ are woven from handspun natural white and brown wools. The hands of Christ have broken fingers to represent an earlier practice in Chimayó, in which villagers threw fragments of the wooden fingers into the fields to insure a good harvest.

The Vallero is also undergoing a renaissance in the hands of contemporary weavers. *Which Way to El Valle* by Irvin Trujillo is a variation of the Trampas Vallero, characterized by its five-star placement: a central star flanked by four stars, one in each corner of the weaving. In place of the usual center star, Trujillo has substituted a Saltillo diamond to illustrate that the Saltillo design historically precedes the Vallero. The diamond is bordered by two eight-pointed Vallero stars. The tulip border in *Which Way to El Valle* is based on the pattern developed by Martina Montoya in the late nineteenth century and traditionally woven by the Trujillo family. Of the other sisters in the Montoya family who popularized the Vallero style, Patricia Montoya wove zigzag designs in her borders.

The Falling Stars (see page 43) by Karen Martínez presents another variation of the Vallero. A central eight-pointed star is the focal point of the weaving, but in place of the four corner stars, Martínez has woven an additional forty-two stars, placing them on a stylized step design. The background vertical lines are derived from Saltillo patterns. Blending her dyes of cochineal and indigo to gradated shades, Martínez achieves a three-dimensional effect in the weaving.

This pictorial by Irene López, which took close to a year to complete, was inspired by the crucifix of Nuestro Señor de Esquípulas at the Santuario de Chimayó where López and her family have made pilgrimages for years. It measures 82 by 43^1/$_2$ inches.

Irvin Trujillo 'begins' this Vallero weaving with a border of Chimayó designs to establish the colors he will use in the rest of the weaving.

Irvin Trujillo weaves while his wife, Lisa, spins at Centinela Traditional Arts in Chimayó

Irvin and Lisa Trujillo are among the youngest of the weaver/owners in Chimayó. They started Centinela Traditional Arts with Irvin's family in 1982, following their wedding and Lisa's college graduation at age twenty. Irvin learned to weave at age ten from his father, Jacobo O. "Jake" Trujillo, and is a seventh-generation Chimayó weaver, although he spent some years away from Chimayó working as a civil engineer. Lisa, an Anglo, learned weaving from Irvin and her father-in-law so she and Irvin could return to Chimayó to start their business. She has gone on to distinguish herself as a master weaver. They have won more than twenty-five major awards for their weaving, and their work has appeared in over thirty publications. The couple oversees the production of Centinela Traditional Arts, which includes ten contract weavers, two full-time sewers, and three salespersons.

Irvin and Lisa Trujillo, skilled in traditional Rio Grande and Chimayó designs, are also renowned for their contemporary interpretations of classic designs, which Irvin describes as "post-war Rio Grande weaving." *Todas las Madres* (All of the Mothers) by Lisa Trujillo, for example, is reminiscent of nineteenth-century Saltillos with its central lozenge, background pattern, and detailed border (see page 5). However, the repeating motif of bows is unusual and innovative, as is the soft palette composed of handspun wool and natural dyes of cochineal, indigo, madder root, and black walnut hulls.

La Vereda by Irvin Trujillo is based upon two inverted triangles. Between them are five bands with a different object on each band. Inspired to weave this piece as he was turning forty, Trujillo has charted the passage of time through cars: the sports car is man at a young age; the truck represents middle age; and the hearse is old age. The space ship symbolizes death and going beyond time, and the dove is beyond death. A tree of life at the top of the weaving balances a stylized bird at the bottom.

§ § §

Once a predominantly male occupation, Rio Grande weaving has expanded to include just as many, if not more, talented female weavers. Doña Agueda Martínez and Teresa Archuleta-Sagel stand at the two ends of twentieth-century Hispanic weaving, as do Irvin Trujillo and his father, Jake, representing a tradition that goes back four hundred years. While production work still sustains many weavers, the individual artist has emerged in the last quarter of a century to take Rio Grande weaving to a new level of excellence.

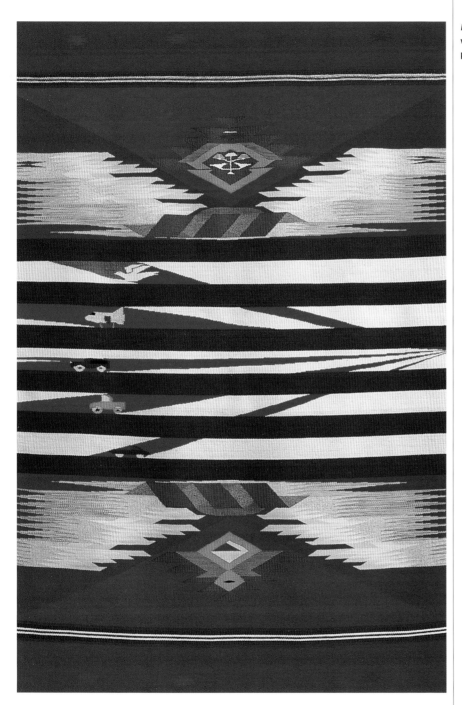

La vereda means "path" or "lane." In this weaving, Irvin Trujillo has charted man's path through life.

Chapter 2

Woodworking and Furniture Making

A view of the doors at San José de Gracia de Las Trampas Church in Las Trampas

Completed in 1760, Las Trampas church is one of three northern New Mexican churches dating from the eighteenth century (the other two are Holy Cross Church in Santa Cruz and San Miguel Church in Santa Fe). Wooden structures original to the church include the door frame and lintel. In the center of the lintel is a figure of an angel, on either side of which is the signature of the woodworker in Spanish; the translation is "Made by the hand of Nicolás de Apodaca." The vertical door frames are also original and have been hand-carved with a rope design. The wooden balcony was restored in 1967 (with the rest of the church), and the spindles were modeled after one remaining spindle, most probably dating from the nineteenth century. The current doors were made in the mid to late nineteenth century, and the wooden bell towers are early twentieth century. The church was designated a historic site in 1967.

N THE 1980S, THE "SANTA FE STYLE" BECAME a national rage, popping up all over the country in pastel desert colors, adobe architecture, the ubiquitous wooden coyote, and cactus and petroglyph motifs painted on everything from clothing to furniture to stoneware. In yet another cycle of appreciation for the Southwest's Native American and Hispanic cultures, tourists flocked to Santa Fe for a glimpse into the romantic past of that region and to take home a memento of the West, much as their predecessors had done one hundred years earlier, when the railroad first reached New Mexico's capital. In 1986, Christine Mather and Sharon Woods published *Santa Fe Style,* focusing on the "pure and simple" lines of adobe architecture, the spare but solid furnishings inherited from the Spanish Colonial era, and the exquisite wood carving found in the interiors of New Mexico's churches and homes.

The Santa Fe style that Mather and Woods documented is rooted in a style of architecture that has variously been called Pueblo Revival or Spanish-Pueblo Revival, which emerged in the second decade of the twentieth century due to efforts by artists, historians, and architects to preserve the city's historical architecture. In a reaction to the Anglo-American influences of the Territorial Period (1846–1912), which had dotted the landscape with pitched tin roofs and brick and frame homes, historic preservationists called for a return to the flat-roofed multi-storied adobe architecture of New Mexico's Pueblo and Spanish cultures. Accompanying the "revival" in traditional adobe architecture, which inspired Santa Fe's Museum of Fine Arts built in 1917, among other public buildings, was a renewed appreciation of Spanish Colonial furniture and woodworking, which spans four hundred years in New Mexico.

Page 58
Antonio Archuleta has constructed this bench with floral motifs on the side panels that have been hand-tinted to produce the soft colors.

Page 59, top
Luis Tapia and his son Sergio Tapia collaborated on this trastero. The blue-green and terra-cotta colors are reminiscent of the polychrome chests imported from Michoácan and painted pieces from Spanish Colonial New Mexico.

Page 59, bottom
This chest by George Sandoval illustrates the popular rosette pattern and scallop design carved on Spanish Colonial furniture. Estate inventories from the eighteenth and nineteenth centuries list the number of chests in various households, most of which were used to store textiles prized by the settlers.

Taos Pueblo, one of the oldest continually inhabited settlements in North America. The Spanish introduced the outdoor *horno,* a beehive-shaped adobe oven for baking bread, to the pueblos. Moorish in origin, hornos are used today throughout Pueblo and Spanish villages.

61

Known for his skill in hand-plastering, as well as furniture making and woodworking, Wilberto Miera constructs these doors with a cut-out Peñasco-style design in the middle panel. Miera often incorporates Native American motifs into the opposite side of his doors to reflect the multi-cultural influences upon Hispanic furniture styles.

Furniture making can be traced back to the 1598 colonization of New Mexico under Juan de Oñate. In their insightful and comprehensive survey, *New Mexican Furniture—1600–1940,* Lonn Taylor and Dessa Bokides document that one *carpintero* accompanied Oñate's expedition, while six other settlers brought with them woodworking tools, including adzes, augers, axes, chisels, nails, a crowbar, and a wagon-maker's hammer. The immediate tasks for carpenters in the seventeenth century were to build homes and churches. Within the Rio Grande pueblos, the Spanish encountered a workforce already familiar with constructing dwellings out of adobe by mixing mud with straw and applying it with a *puddling* technique. The Spanish introduced the technology of molding adobe into bricks in wooden troughs. With axes, they cut down large ponderosa pine trees that were then stripped of bark and shaped into *vigas,* the supporting beams for the roofs of their dwellings. Smaller poles of peeled juniper or aspen called *latillas* were placed over the vigas. Carpenters also made wooden doors for missions and homes, a new invention for the Pueblo tribes, who had used ladders to enter their homes from the rooftops. Other Spanish contributions to architecture included a fireplace and chimney for cooking, as opposed to the pit hole Pueblo tribes had used.

Because virtually everything Spanish was destroyed during the Pueblo Revolt, there is scant evidence of what the early Spanish Colonial homes looked like. Inventories dating from 1660 list furnishings that were imported from Mexico and Spain, none of which survived. The New Mexican–style home evolved in the late Colonial period, and the interiors were generally spare. Built-in adobe *bancos* around the exterior of the central room provided seating, as well as a sleeping surface. Wall niches housed saints *(santos),* while shelved niches with wooden shutters *(alacenas* or wall cupboards) provided storage. Hanging shelves *(repisas)* added another space for possessions, as did the handmade wooden chests *(cajas).* Small portable stools called *tarimas* were also common. From the Moors, the Spanish had inherited the custom of sitting on the floor on pillows or small stools and cushions, and this tradition was easily incorporated into Spanish New Mexico. Although iron hinges, locks, and nails were available, they were precious and used sparingly, dictating a *mortise-and-tenon* construction, in which an extension of a piece of wood (the tenon) is carved to fit into a rectangular cavity (the mortise) to make a joint.

Government documents and the memoirs of Fray Alonso de Benavides, a Franciscan prelate assigned to New Mexico in 1625, note that the Spanish had taught Native Americans woodworking, enlisting their labor for building mission churches. Woodworkers at Pecos Pueblo continued to make furniture throughout the eighteenth century, and Cochiti Pueblo has been identified as another center of furniture making. After the reconquest (1692–1696), the demand for skilled woodworkers was sufficiently high to employ dozens of carpenters by the end of the eighteenth century. In the absence of formal guilds for woodworkers, carpenters passed their skills on to immediate and extended family members, who in turn became specialized in furniture making.

This re-creation of Governor Armijo's room at the Palace of the Governors Museum in Santa Fe illustrates the furnishings of nineteenth-century New Mexican homes. A wooden chandelier, or *araña,* and two tin sconces provide light. The floor is covered with a hand-woven *jerga.* The chest on a tall stand is a painted chest from Michoácan, Mexico. Above the chest is an *alacena,* or wall cupboard. The table and chairs are made with mortise-and-tenon joinery.

This Spanish Colonial writing desk by Ramón José López is made from hand-adzed pine, natural pigments, and buffalo hide. The drawers are painted with pomegranate designs. The writing surface contains a Sacred Heart surrounded by angels, and a small *retablo* of San Camilo de Lelis in the center niche. The hand-pierced sterling silver pulls on the exterior (also made by López) are modeled after the double-headed eagle crest of the Hapsburgs, rulers of Spain from 1516 to 1700.

Chests were the most popular form of furniture made during the Spanish Colonial period, because of their portability and convenience for storage. Board chests were constructed of hand-adzed pine panels fitted together with *dovetail* joints. In dovetailing, the tenon is flared and fit into a matching mortise to form a tight right-angle joint. The pegged mortise-and-tenon joint was used for framed chests, in which wooden panels were slipped into channels formed by vertical stiles and horizontal rails. Additional strips of wood embellished the false framed chest to imitate a framed chest. Decorative motifs carved in relief on the panels of board chests included rosettes, vines, pomegranates, crosses, and lions. Painted chests were also common, many of which were imported into New Mexico from Michoacán, Mexico.

Within the category of chests are *harineros* (large flour chests), that came into existence around 1800 with the increasing number of water mills, which replaced the hand-grinding of corn and grain. Constructed on legs to keep them out of reach of insects and rodents, harineros were larger than ordinary chests to store greater quantities of ground flour. Other chests were also placed on legs, which were sometimes embellished with chip-carving derived from Moorish designs. By the end of the eighteenth century, New Mexican furniture makers had developed the unique style of extending the legs of their chests. In her thorough review of Spanish Colonial furniture in *Spanish New Mexico,* Donna Pierce speculates that the chest-on-leg style was influenced by the Mexican and Spanish writing desks, now called *vargueños,* which resemble a chest when closed. When open, the front panel drops down to provide a platform for writing. The interior of the vargueño contains numerous compartments for writing materials and documents.

Antonio Archuleta's chest on a scissor stand is hand-carved with traditional Castilian designs of opposing lions, shells, and pomegranates. Constructed with dovetail joints, the designs are carved in high relief by chiseling away the surrounding wood.

The carved finials of this Spanish armchair are imitated in the curve of the arms. The front stretcher has a rosette pattern in the middle and scalloped edges.

Antonio Archuleta has constructed this bench after the style of his mentor and colleague, Elidio Gonzáles. The spindles on the back of the bench are all hand-carved.

Chairs in colonial New Mexico were modeled after their Spanish prototypes with sturdy, straightforward lines and constructed with mortise-and-tenon joinery. Armchairs were sometimes made with a broad front stretcher—a horizontal wooden bar extending between the two front legs—upon which designs were carved or cut out. Chip-carving, geometric and floral designs, and Pueblo step or cloud designs (also a popular motif in Moorish art) adorn both armchairs and side chairs.

The majority of Spanish Colonial furniture is made from ponderosa pine, a soft wood indigenous to northern New Mexico. The tendency of ponderosa to split and fracture influenced the construction and designs of historic furniture. Wooden dowels were more effective in strengthening the mortise-and-tenon joinery than nails, which could further cleave the wood. Similarly, simple carved motifs and cut-outs were easier to execute than ornate baroque patterns, balancing the uncomplicated lines of the furniture.

In addition to chests and chairs, Spanish Colonial furniture makers built *bancos* or benches for use at home. In the second half of the nineteenth century, wealthy New Mexicans had their own benches made for church so they could be seated. Before Bishop Lamy introduced permanent pews, churches were bare except for the altar. Parishioners knelt or stood on a dirt floor during mass. Benches provided space for many family members and presented furniture makers with an opportunity to exhibit their skills. The back frequently displayed cut-out designs and handsome carving, while the border of the front apron was hewn in a complementary design. *Splats,* thin vertical panels, added another design element to the back of the bench between the seat and the top rail, or to the bottom between the skirt and the bottom rail. Scallop designs and step motifs were popular borders.

To this trastero made of ponderosa pine, Greg Flores adds innovative touches such as longer legs, an enlarged scallop crest, and carved finials suggestive of Moorish turrets. The cut-out panels of the doors are a variation of the classic Peñasco design—an elongated hourglass figure popular among furniture makers from the Taos/Peñasco area. The introduction of milled lumber and frame saws made such curvilinear designs possible in the second half of the nineteenth century.

For storage, woodworkers built *armarios* (tall cabinets, now known as *trasteros*), either with solid doors or with open fretwork on the door's upper half. Before glass became more available in the nineteenth century, colonists covered their windows with wooden grills for protection, a tradition inherited from the Moors. The same spindles used in the window grills were translated into trasteros, among other designs, so the owner could see the contents inside the cabinet. Decoration was generally limited to the front of the trasteros, and the tops were fitted with cornices, such as carved rosettes. Some trasteros were also gessoed and painted.

The nineteenth century brought many changes to New Mexico, not the least of which was an influx of Anglo-American immigrants, who began settling in the territory after the opening of the Santa Fe Trail in 1821. By the 1850s, a number of non-Hispanic furniture makers had set up shop, producing styles that were then in vogue in the eastern United States. The Santa Fe Trail also provided a way to get new carpenters' tools and manufactured hardware, such as door hinges and locks for chests, and nails and screws. Taylor and Bokides cite the frame saw and the molding plane as the two most innovative tools that changed the direction of furniture making in the nineteenth century. The first made it possible for woodworkers to make circles and curves in decorative molding; the second allowed for more control over edges and for shaping recessed or relieved surfaces on molding.

The Santa Fe Trail also brought in supplies for the United States Army, which was a permanent fixture in New Mexico after 1846. In 1847, the army built the first sawmill in Santa Fe to provide lumber for their forts. Milled lumber, readily accessible by the 1870s, was more easily decorated than the thick hand-hewn pine timbers of the Colonial period, and the painstaking labor of mortise-and-tenon and dovetail joinery was replaced by the convenient nail. Not all techniques changed, but the Hispanic woodworker now had to compete with Anglo-American furniture makers and a changing market.

Greg Flores in front of his templates in his Taos studio

Greg Flores has developed a unique style in furniture making characterized by purity of form and simplicity in design. While he considers himself a traditionalist—he uses mortise-and-tenon joinery, for example—he is cautious about not replicating the past. Instead, he adds his own interpretations to classic designs, painting some of his pieces in bright blues and reds or exaggerating certain elements to make his pieces unique. Known for the clean work of his cut-out designs, he originated the four-petal flower design that has become popular in contemporary Hispanic furniture.

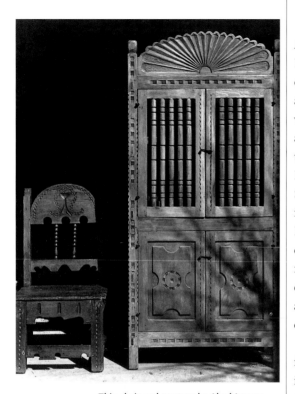

This chair and trastero by Abad Lucero are made with mortise-and-tenon joinery. The spindles are hand-carved and the frame of the trastero is decorated with a chip-carved design.

Taylor and Bokides argue persuasively that the immigrant Anglo-American population introduced new categories of furniture to New Mexico—daybeds, bureaus, desks, bookshelves, washstands, and different types of tables—and that these new styles appealed to the more affluent Hispanics, who combined the comfort of such furnishings with their traditional pieces. In the last half of the nineteenth century, a new market for furniture evolved, forcing the Spanish furniture maker to adapt his style and technology to the demands of a new consumer. Decorative moldings replaced much of the hand-chiseled carving of the Spanish Colonial era, and cut-out patterns and scrollwork, made infinitely easier with the frame saw, embellished daybeds and trasteros. However, by the 1890s, the market for handmade furniture had dwindled dramatically because of mass-produced pieces imported by the railroad. Even with the advanced tools, the individual furniture maker couldn't compete with the factories of the East, and like other handcrafted arts, furniture making receded into the hands of a few isolated carpinteros in the northern New Mexico villages.

The "revival" of Spanish Colonial furniture took place in the first two decades of the twentieth century, in conjunction with the revival in Pueblo-style architecture. Ironically, Anglo-Americans rather than Hispanics initially designed and built furniture for the revival buildings and later for private homes. Members of the Taos and Santa Fe art colonies—notably Nicholai Fechin, Josef Bakos, and William Penhallow Henderson—produced many pieces of furniture based on early prototypes they also collected. Their interest in New Mexico's material culture was shared by other artists, writers, and collectors, who found the simplicity of handcrafted art from the Colonial past a welcome antidote to mass-produced goods churned out by the industrial age.

Under the auspices of the Spanish Colonial Arts Society, Hispanic artisans were encouraged to produce traditional crafts, which they exhibited and sold at annual fiestas beginning in 1926. Other sales outlets for craftspeople were the society's Spanish Arts Shop and the Native Market, where furniture was the number-one seller. Furniture for the shops was provided by individual artisans, some of whom were students at the El Rito Normal School, which had initiated a vocational program dedicated to Hispanic crafts in 1925. While basically a teacher-training institute, the El Rito school anticipated other vocational programs established in New Mexico during the WPA era to teach traditional crafts to Hispanics. These programs provided artisans with an income during the depression, while they kept alive the art forms of the Spanish Colonial period. Much of the furniture produced in the 1930s was commissioned for public buildings, although enough collectors also bought furniture for their homes to once again employ dozens of furniture makers who sold their work at the Native Market.

Part of the training materials produced by the state's Department of Vocational Education included pamphlets on the crafts. The *Spanish Colonial Furniture Bulletin* (1933) consisted of three dozen or so illustrations of early furniture pieces with measurements and notes about construction. The bulletin was edited and reissued in 1984 by William Wroth as *Furniture from the Hispanic Southwest*. Then, as now, the *Bulletin* provided a detailed guide of historic styles for furniture makers to follow.

World War II marked another turning point for Hispanic furniture makers, many of whom retrained to work in the West Coast aeronautics industry as pattern makers, welders, and sheet-metal workers. After the war, more jobs were available in those fields in the growing urban centers of New Mexico, attracting artisans away from their villages. In contrast to the more expansive market for furniture in the 1930s, the demand for Spanish Colonial Revival furniture after the war remained confined to a few wealthy patrons and occasional public commissions, leading once again to a diminution in the crafts.

Furniture in the post-war period tended to follow the classic designs of traditional Spanish Colonial pieces, made by only a handful of furniture makers. Abad Lucero (b. 1909) had taught furniture making at the Taos and Mora Vocational Schools during the WPA era and served as manager of furniture making for the Native Market in Santa Fe. He later started a furniture shop of his own with his student Elidio Gonzáles in Taos and today continues handcrafting pieces with traditional mortise-and-tenon joinery and hand-adzed wood in Albuquerque. From 1945 to 1988, Gonzáles (d. 1988) operated El Artesano de Taos, establishing a reputation for carving classic Castilian designs, which he passed on to his apprentice, Antonio Archuleta, who began working with him in

Abad Lucero in his studio at age eighty-seven, Albuquerque

Born in 1909, Abad Lucero's career in woodworking spans most of the twentieth century. He worked as an apprentice cabinetmaker from 1928 to 1931 at the Santa Fe Tile and Pine Shop. A self-taught furniture maker, he learned many of the Spanish Colonial styles from drawings given to him by architect Bill Lumpkins. Lumpkins later reproduced the drawings for bulletins published by the New Mexico State Department of Vocational Education and distributed to furniture makers from 1933 to 1939. In 1933, Lucero was hired by the Department of Vocational Education to teach furniture making, wrought-iron work, and carving. In this same period he founded his own furniture-making shop in Taos with Elidio Gonzáles. In 1949, Lucero moved to Albuquerque, where he lives and works today. Dedicated to preserving the traditional styles and techniques of Spanish Colonial furniture, Lucero has taught several generations of furniture makers over the last sixty years. His work is characterized by generous proportions, mortise-and-tenon joinery, hand-adzed wood, strong lines, and traditional design motifs.

A functional sideboard with drawers and shelved cupboards, this piece by Fred Romero is unmistakably New Mexican, with the carved rosettes on the doors and the scalloped crest on top, which Romero has elongated to suggest the rays of the sun.

1962. George Sandoval (b. 1930), a graduate of the El Rito Normal School, who learned woodworking from his grandfather, is another pioneer of the "quiet years," beginning his career in furniture making in 1950. Still active today, he has taught many woodworkers, including his son Chris Sandoval, who owns and makes furniture for Artisans of the Desert in Albuquerque. These and other individuals sustained the art of Spanish Colonial furniture making during the middle decades of the twentieth century, when the trend in architecture and furniture styles was typified by the sleek modernism of chrome and leather.

By the 1970s, the American Craft movement had taken hold, inspiring a new appreciation of handcrafted arts across the country. In New Mexico, this movement coincided with a renewed interest among Hispanic artists in the crafts of their Spanish heritage. In 1975, Luis Tapia was the first Hispanic artist to exhibit furniture at Spanish Market, encouraged to do so by Alan Vedder, a collector and author of *Furniture of Spanish New Mexico*. Also an accomplished artist and image maker, or *santero* (see chapter 4), Tapia has built and restored Spanish Colonial furniture for more than twenty years. In his exploration of early techniques for making furniture and santos, Tapia discovered that his forebears had used vivid colors for their painted pieces, which he has introduced into his own furniture. Color has also become the hallmark of the work of several other contemporary furniture makers, notably Greg Flores.

Innovations in carved designs also distinguish contemporary Hispanic furniture. Wilberto Miera's trastero, for example, combines classic designs from Native American, Spanish, and Moorish traditions—all of which influenced Spanish Colonial furniture. On the side panels, the rosette is bordered on either side by diamond-shaped step designs found on Navajo textiles. The doors include the Spanish cross and rosettes, while the hand-adzed, carved spindles derive from Moorish designs. Miera's versatility comes from his years of working as a carpenter for the exhibitions department at the Museum of New Mexico, where he also had an opportunity to study Spanish Colonial pieces. The trastero, which is over 8 feet tall, is constructed with mortise-and-tenon joinery and is hand-carved from ponderosa pine.

The scallop design on the crest of this trastero by Wilberto Miera—a popular motif in Hispanic furniture—represents the shell carried by pilgrims of St. James the Apostle that has its roots in medieval Spain. For centuries, pilgrims have journeyed to the church of Santiago de Compostela, where the remains of St. James are reported to be buried. Formerly, they were given a document granting them religious pardons and remission from purgatory. Returning pilgrims attached scallop shells to their clothing as a symbol that they had reached their destination, since scallops were a rarity in the rest of Spain. Sojourners today receive a certificate in Latin conferring upon them the status of pilgrim.

Similarly, the *carreta* by Lawrence Quintana illustrates an imaginative interpretation of the traditional two-wheeled cart. Transportation in rural New Mexico has always been tenuous. During the Colonial period, all-wood carts were constructed to carry loads of hay and to haul goods short distances. Colonial wagon wheels were made out of cottonwood, a harder wood than pine, while the body was generally constructed of pine.

Quintana's carreta exemplifies the versatility of contemporary Hispanic furniture making. In an era when mass-produced Santa Fe–style furniture competes with handcrafted pieces, Hispanic artisans have had to adapt their ideas and techniques to new styles of furniture. Traditional styles are translated into modern forms, such as the credenza by Fred Romero, which is based on a Shaker style but incorporates New Mexican design elements. A step design embellishes the lip of the buffet and is repeated underneath the cabinet and on the bottom shelf. Chip carving completes the piece, which has an extended-peg mortise-and-tenon construction.

Ecclesiastical woodworking is another area in which contemporary furniture makers express their multifaceted skills, at the same time perpetuating the traditions of their ancestors, making altars, tabernacles, altar tables, armchairs, and stations of the cross for churches in New Mexico and other states. Roberto Lavadie, for example, commissioned by Our Lady of Guadalupe Church in Taos, made the altar, railings, table, chairs, and carved moldings for the sanctuary. The massiveness of the *reredos* (altar screen) is reflected in the large rosette and shell decorations on the sides and top, which are repeated as framing decorations in the individual bays. Spiral-carved legs and columns are duplicated in the vertical splats of the chairs. On the altar table, Lavadie has carved two doves on top of the ornate floral motif.

SOY TU MADRE. NUNCA TE PREOC

For the altar screen at Our Lady of Guadalupe Church in Taos, Roberto Lavadie invited members of the communities surrounding the church to each paint one of the panels for the screen. The central portrait of Our Lady of Guadalupe includes four scenes that recount her miracles.

Lawrence Quintana hand carved the spindles of this cart from single blocks of ponderosa pine that extend through the top rail. The entire vehicle is assembled with mortise-and-tenon construction, and without glue or metal.

The thirteenth Station of the Cross, painted by Marie Romero Cash and framed by Robert Montoya, St. Francis Cathedral, Santa Fe. Montoya's design for the frames of the fourteen stations of the cross is based on seventeenth-century Spanish Colonial styles, with two-strand carved spiral columns and scallop pediments. Chip-carved crosses decorate the sides of the frame. Marie Romero Cash painted all of the stations.

Santa María de la Paz Church in Santa Fe has perhaps commissioned more work by Hispanic artists than any other church in New Mexico. More than thirty santeros, weavers, tinworkers, straw appliqué artists, and woodworkers have created the altars, images, and furnishings. Lavadie and Robert Montoya, who often collaborate on large projects, designed and crafted the altar, a chest for religious documents, the lectern, and the cantor's desk. In 1996, Montoya won a competition sponsored by the St. Francis Cathedral in Santa Fe to design and construct the frames for the fourteen stations of the cross painted by santera Marie Romero Cash. Lavadie assisted with the carving of the stations, which are constructed from Philippine mahogany and weigh approximately seventy pounds each.

Four styles of chairs

Carving elevates even the simplest of furniture pieces, such as chairs, to an artistic level. These four chairs all exhibit the Spanish Colonial elements of hand-carved spindles, shell crests, and decorated front stretchers. All are constructed with mortise-and-tenon joinery from native pine, yet each displays unique characteristics. Going counterclockwise from upper left, David C'de Baca has chip-carved nineteenth-century Pueblo motifs of cornstalks and cloud designs on the frame of his chair. Tim Roybal adds a rope design to the posts of his chair, carving a scallop design around the skirt and bottom rails. A deeply carved rosette anchors the front stretcher of Federico Prudencio's chair, while a scroll pattern is used for the side bottom rails. Similarly, the popular scallop design is the primary design motif in Lawrence Quintana's chair.

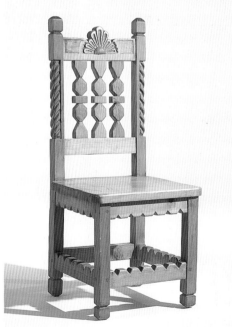

Another example of furniture made for the church is David C'de Baca's painted chest based on a nineteenth-century vestment chest found in the Ranchos de Taos Church. One interior compartment was used for storing the chalice for Holy Communion; the other larger compartment stored altar coverings and the priest's garments. Made of sugar pine, the chest panels are set in a groove, like framed chests, and the wood is hand-adzed. The scallop designs are executed with a compass in the same manner the historic furniture makers worked, and the chest is finished with three coats of beeswax to protect the painted finish. Of the original Spanish Colonial furniture, which he has studied and which his own work mirrors, C'de Baca says, "it is so pretty and simple and not overdone."

David C'de Baca outside his studio, La Cienega

David C'de Baca has distinguished himself among contemporary Hispanic furniture makers for his strict adherence to traditional styles and techniques of the Spanish Colonial period. His paints are water-based natural pigments, for example, and he uses beeswax to seal his pieces. Working primarily in ponderosa and sugar pine and hand-adzing the wood, he uses the compass and chisel that the historic furniture maker would have used to lay out and carve his designs. Largely self-taught, he studied Spanish Colonial styles in museums and publications, as well as in the work of his father, Tomás C'de Baca (who died when David was five), a furniture maker and instructor during the WPA era. Also skilled in contemporary styles, he gets many of his ideas from designs on window grates, for example, adapting the motifs to his distinctive furniture.

David C'de Baca gessoed and painted the exterior of this chest in the style of Molleno, the nineteenth-century santero who painted the original.

Chapter 3

Straw Appliqué
and
Tin Craft

Tin and straw appliqué crosses decorate a corner of Our Lady of Guadalupe Chapel in Velarde. These crosses and frames are gifts to Eulogio and Zoraida Ortega, donated over the years by people who have visited their chapel and been inspired by their devotion to Our Lady of Guadalupe.

Page 78
This mirror by Angelina Delgado Martínez illustrates her unique stamp work and embossing.

Page 79, top
This cross by Paula Rodríguez includes some of her favorite saints (on the vertical bar beneath the nativity scene): Our Lady of Guadalupe, the Holy Child of Atocha, and Our Lady of the Miraculous Medal. Prayer cards are often her models for the shapes and attributes of the saints.

Page 79, bottom
In this box, Jimmy Romero employs the combed-glass technique, which creates a wavy-line pattern in the painted glass panels.

OR MORE THAN TWO HUNDRED YEARS (1598–1846), the Spanish colonists in New Mexico depended upon their own talents and the land for survival. They built adobe homes from mud and straw bricks, raised sheep for food and wool, and made their own furniture and household utensils from trees they cut down themselves. From the same native woods, they fashioned agricultural tools for plowing. Their labor raised the walls of village churches, and the artists among them furnished those churches with the carved and painted saints of their Catholic faith.

Self-reliant by temperament and necessity, the Spanish colonist found beauty in the humblest of materials—such as straw and corn husks—developing the art of straw appliqué by the end of the eighteenth century to decorate crosses, nichos, candle sconces, chests, armoires, and picture frames. The origin of straw appliqué work in New Mexico is uncertain, but it appears to have been inspired by a decorative technique called *marquetry,* in which complex patterns of wood, shell, ivory, and occasionally metals are applied to wood, either through inlay or mosaic overlay. For inlay, the pattern is placed in an indentation made in the wood. For mosaic overlay, pre-cut materials are glued directly on a surface and ground down to one smooth surface that is then polished.

In Spain, the art of mosaic became firmly established during the long Moorish occupation (711–1492), especially in southern Spain. Donna Pierce says in *Spanish New Mexico:* "Marquetry work from this area is characterized by intricate geometric patterning with a predominance of star and chevron motifs similar to those seen on New Mexican straw work." In the absence of rare woods and imported materials, Spanish artisans used indigenous materials like straw to embellish their furniture. Examples of marquetry decoration most probably were imported into New Mexico from Mexico, where the technique had been introduced by the Spanish in the sixteenth century. By the end of the eighteenth century, Pierce notes, the technique of marquetry using straw and corn husks had become a popular decorative art in Mexico.

Besides the Hispanic-Moresque influence on marquetry designs, trade between Mexico and the Orient during the Spanish

These crosses by Jimmy Trujillo exhibit the star designs, popular in Spanish Colonial work, as well as geometric and floral motifs reminiscent of intricate marquetry patterns. Trujillo is known for the luminescent surface of his crosses, achieved by varnishing them with resin.

**Paula and Eliseo Rodríguez
doing straw appliqué at their
kitchen table**

When Eliseo Rodríguez was asked to recreate the art of straw appliqué in the 1930s, he recalls, "There was nothing written at the time about the technique. There was a small pamphlet by E. Boyd on the history of the art form coming from North Africa to Spain to the New World, but nothing else." After trial and error, combined with research into Spanish Colonial art forms, Rodríguez recreated the techniques his ancestors had used over one hundred years earlier. Paula became an avid student and researcher as well, working alongside her husband.

Deeply religious—the couple start their day with prayers and the rosary—Eliseo and Paula express their devotion to God in figurative crosses based on the life of Christ and the saints. Eliseo's profound knowledge of the Bible comes from his own faith and the years of research he did to complete the largest religious art commission ever given to a New Mexican artist: the fifteen-panel stations of the cross for Our Lady of Grace Catholic Church in Castro Valley, California. Each station measures 4 by 12 feet. Painted in oils, the project took eight years to complete. After its completion, Rodríguez painted a smaller version of the stations to donate to the Penitente Morada in Córdova.

Of their children and grandchildren to whom they have taught the craft of straw appliqué, Vicki Rodríguez stands out for the exquisite miniaturism of her designs. She began doing straw appliqué in 1981 during a year of recovering from back surgery, watching her parents work daily at the kitchen table and then trying it herself. A schoolteacher by profession, Vicki was able to study further with her parents through the master apprentice program funded by the National Endowment for the Arts, becoming as distinguished for her figurative work as for her floral designs.

Colonial period introduced other examples of mosaic work to the New World. Mosaic overlay in jewelry was also an established practice among the indigenous peoples of Mexico and New Mexico, who had traded shells and turquoise with each other since prehistoric times and may have applied the same techniques required in mosaic to their own straw appliqué work. Geometric designs in Spanish Colonial straw appliqué are similar to Pueblo Indian motifs and to Mexican and Spanish sources, suggesting what Pierce terms "an artistic interface between the two cultures...which reinforced the use of similar motifs in local straw work."

The art of straw appliqué is composed of several steps. The base object is first constructed from wood and then sanded and painted. In Colonial New Mexico, popular colors included black (derived from burnt lamp oil) and vermilion and indigo (trade items imported from Mexico). A glue mixture of piñon pitch diluted with grain alcohol was then applied to the painted object, onto which designs made from cut pieces of corn husks or wheat straw were placed. Before being cut to the desired shape, the straw shaft was split and flattened. A final varnish of resin,

On decorating his crosses, Eliseo Rodríguez says, "It's like a prayer for me. I talk to the saints while I'm making them." This cross portrays the life of Christ in more than a dozen tableaux.

Paula Rodríguez decorates this frame for Eliseo Rodríguez's station of the cross with straw appliqué, designating the number of the station (8) on the rosette above the frame.

Plaques have become a popular backdrop for narrative stories. In this plaque, Paula Rodríguez portrays St. Francis and his devotion to nature. She uses wheat and barley straw from Michigan.

also derived from pine pitch, sealed the design into place and protected it and the base wood from deterioration. The contrast of the golden color of the wheat or corn with the darker base created the illusion of gold, prompting scholar E. Boyd to refer to straw appliqué as the "poor man's gilding."

Straw appliqué designs in Colonial New Mexico were primarily geometric and floral, reflecting the design aesthetic of southern Spain. By the middle of the nineteenth century, however, straw appliqué had died out, according to Boyd, because the introduction of tin provided a more durable material for decoration. With occasional exceptions, it would not be until the WPA era that the art form would be revived by Eliseo Rodríguez (b. 1915).

Rodríguez, a woodworker and painter of singular talent—he had received a scholarship to the Santa Fe Art School at age fourteen—applied to become a teacher in the New Mexico Federal Art Project in 1936 in the wake of the Great Depression to support himself and his wife, Paula, whom he had married in 1935. The director of the project, Russell Vernon Hunter, was also an artist with a strong interest in New Mexico's Spanish Colonial past. Recognizing Rodríguez's diverse talents, Hunter asked him to experiment with reproducing straw appliqué to revive the craft. Over the last sixty years, Eliseo Rodríguez has applied his talents as a painter to his straw appliqué, cutting the shafts of wheat and barley into razor-thin sheets to create the shimmering effect of darker and lighter shades of gold. He introduced figures into straw appliqué, recreating entire biblical stories on a single cross. (To date, no figurative work from the historic period has been uncovered; only geometric and floral designs in straw appliqué have survived.) Rodríguez also increased the scale of straw appliqué work from traditionally small objects to crosses as large as eight by four feet.

Paula Rodríguez is also known for her figurative portrayals of religious stories on both plaques and crosses. Based on the birth of Christ, the design of her cross (see page 79) is constructed from the center nativity scene out to the scenes of the shepherds on one side and the three kings on the other. The Holy Trinity looks down from above, and the star in the east guides the shepherds and wise men to the manger.

The colors of straw used in this triptych of Our Lady of Guadalupe by Jimmy Trujillo are various shades of gold for the figures, a light pink for the flowers, a deeper red for the Virgin's mantle, and purple for the crescent moon.

Charlie Sánchez Jr. uses color to convey the different themes in his crosses: reds may signify sunset colors and blues and greens are often tied to Pueblo Indian themes. Each cross has a title and is signed with a straw appliqué symbol.

Among contemporary straw artists, the process of preparing the wood for appliqué is as critical as the decoration itself. For smaller pieces, most artists use milled lumber, but for major pieces, artists like Jimmy Trujillo incorporate the Spanish Colonial technique of hand-splitting and adzing ponderosa pine, which is then smoothed with a pocket knife before sanding and painting. Trujillo also uses the black, red, and blue colors of the Spanish Colonial era. For Trujillo, the process of appliqué is more accurately termed *encrusting* straw, because the straw is layered into the resin that covers the wood surface. Like many straw artists, Trujillo gets his wheat straw from a number of sources. He also cultivates a small cornfield to grow different colors of corn for his work.

Crosses remain the preferred canvas for straw appliqué work among contemporary artists. The *Cruz de Santísima Trinidad* by Charlie Sánchez signifies the Trinity in the three crosses coming out of one body, within which are three smaller crosses. The carved rosettes on top of each cross also symbolize the Trinity. The green and rust-colored woods, mixed with the traditional black, add a contemporary touch to the classic chevron and floral designs.

§ § §

Jimmy Trujillo with his daughter Cordilia Marie preparing for Spanish Market, 1992

Jimmy Trujillo credits Charles Carrillo, his nephew by marriage, with introducing him to straw work in 1984. Fascinated by the miniaturism and intricacy of the straw and corn husk designs, Trujillo is responsible for reviving the traditional encrusted straw technique, using piñon resin in place of commercial white glue for fixing the straw to a wooden surface. He seals all of his pieces with a varnish, also derived from piñon pine resin, to produce a high-gloss finish. Trujillo has also pioneered the use of different colors in straw appliqué. He cultivates ornamental corn for the variety of hues in his work: light pink, white variegated with purple, greens, blues, and reds. In addition, he researches and reproduces historic pieces, such as the *arañas* (chandeliers) he made for the Santa María de la Paz Church in Santa Fe. (One definition of *araña* is spider, which refers to the way historic wooden chandeliers dangled from a rope.)

This processional cross by Timothy Valdez was made for the archdiocese in Santa Fe. Straw appliqué crosses also were frequently made for *moradas* (chapter houses of the Penitente Brotherhood). The more elaborate styles had multitiered arms with smaller crosses and were often used for processionals during Easter Week and other religious occasions. Such crosses are also called Penitente crosses. This cross is over 3 feet tall by almost 2 feet wide.

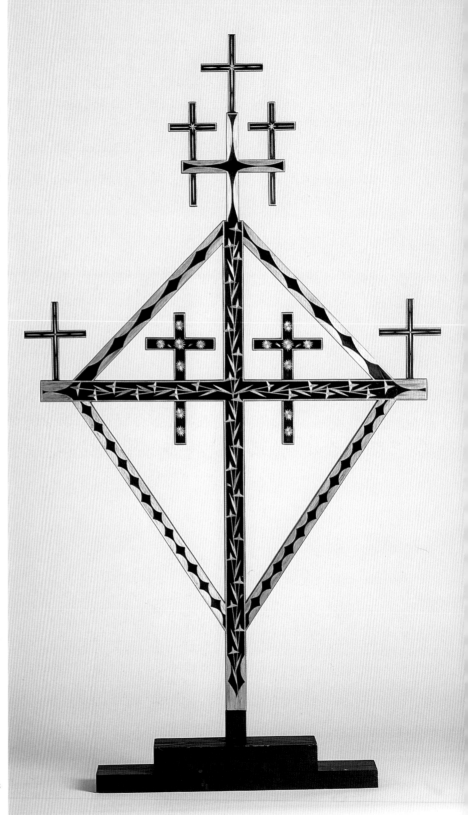

Innovation in design also characterizes Tim Valdez's Penitente cross, with its diamond shape crowned by three crosses representing the Trinity and bisected with multiple crosses on the horizontal brace. Valdez covers the beams of the diamond shape with straw appliqué, letting the design emerge in black from negative space. For the smaller crosses, he reverses the technique, creating his designs in straw appliqué.

Among the popular objects for straw appliqué in both the historic and the contemporary periods are boxes. Silk shawls imported from Mexico into New Mexico in the nineteenth century, states Pierce, were often packed in boxes decorated with elaborate marquetry work, which may have influenced the patterns in New Mexican straw appliqué. In addition to frames and candle sconces, boxes in all sizes are among the utilitarian objects decorated by straw artists.

§ § §

These boxes by Mel Rivera are decorated with hummingbirds and butterflies, as well as delicate floral designs. Rivera cultivates his own wheat straw, letting some of the stalks weather into a deep golden tone that he prefers for his floral designs. He has also popularized the Pueblo step design and the bear in his work.

Framed mirrors and picture frames are popular tin objects made by contemporary tinsmiths. The framed mirror in the back of this collage is by Michael Griego, known for his traditional tinwork style. Next is a mirror constructed in the Santa Fe Federal style by Juan D. Martínez. Characteristic of the rectangular Federal style (ca. 1840–1870) is elaborate stamping and embossing. Side panels are constructed to represent columns, and squared-off corners of the frames frequently exhibit rosette designs. The next picture frame is also by Martínez. Jimmy Martin-Madrid's frame in the front holds a print entitled *The Three Marys*.

These three boxes represent different styles of decorating glass panels. Robert and Annie Romero use wallpaper strips on their music box (back). Senaida Romero embroidered the colcha that adorns her box (left). And Jimmy Romero employs the combed-glass technique, which creates a wavy-line pattern in the paint, for his box (right).

Angelina Delgado Martínez recalls making tin "jingles" by the dozens during the late 1930s with her father, Ildeberto "Eddie" Delgado. They sold these to the Indians under the portal in Santa Fe to use on bags, vests, clothing, and ceremonial dresses. She says that it's possible her grandfather had made the cone tinklers much earlier for sale to Native Americans as well.

If straw appliqué is the "poor man's gold," tinwork is the "poor man's silver." The evolution of tinwork as a decorative art in New Mexico coincided with the American occupation in 1846, when New Mexico became a territory of the United States. Under Brigadier General Stephen Watts Kearny, United States Army troops were garrisoned next to the Palace of the Governors in Santa Fe. Supplies for the troops were transported over the Santa Fe Trail, including "small quantities of window glass for officers' quarters and large tin containers of lard and lamp oil," state Lane Coulter and Maurice Dixon in their comprehensive study, *New Mexican Tinwork—1840–1940*. Tin cans to preserve food were an invention of the early nineteenth century, and the United States Army used the heavy containers (some holding up to five gallons) to transport their foodstuffs. Inventive Hispanic artisans took the cast-off tin cans and used the backings for picture frames (some still carry the label of the packing company). Some containers were transformed into nichos, while others were cut into strips and pieces as decorations for the base object, launching a tradition of tinwork in New Mexico that has endured for more than a century.

Before 1846, tin was not readily available, although tin articles from Mexico and Spain had been imported into Spanish Colonial New Mexico in the seventeenth century, reflecting a long tradition of working the metal in both countries. Trade manifestos and church inventories from the eighteenth century include tin plates and utensils, as well as religious paraphernalia used in the Catholic mass: the wafer box, reliquaries, wine and water goblets, plates for the host. Crosses and crowns for *bultos* (wooden sculptures) were also made from tin.

By the late 1840s, New Mexican craftsmen had begun making candleholders from the army's discarded tin containers, but it wasn't until a decade later that the nascent art form flourished with the influx of religious lithographs, which needed picture frames. Under the influence of Bishop Jean Baptiste Lamy, Coulter and Dixon say, the mostly French priests appointed to New Mexico after 1851 "encouraged the use of the new printed images and discouraged the continued veneration of the old hand-painted retablos." As the demand for original santero art declined, the market for tin frames to mount the mass-produced religious images exploded. Glass had become available over the Santa Fe Trail and was used in tin frames to conserve the prints and for glass-paneled nichos. Decorative wallpaper, also brought into New Mexico after the Santa Fe Trail opened, was placed under glass panels to further embellish tin boxes, crosses, and mirrors.

Coulter and Dixon estimate that between five thousand and ten thousand tin objects were made in a dozen or more regional workshops during the nineteenth century. The most popular objects were directly linked to religion: frames for prints of santos and nichos for bultos. Also in demand were *pantallas* (sconces), *arañas* (chandeliers), *candeleros* (candlesticks), and *faroles* (lanterns), used to illuminate the dark interiors of churches, family chapels, and homes; glass-panel inserts in tin lanterns made outdoor lighting possible as well. Hispanic artisans also made tin cone *tinklers,* popular among Native American tribes for decorating their leather bags and dance aprons. The tools required for nineteenth-century tinwork were few: cutting shears, stamps and punches for surface decoration, hammers, and a soldering iron to join the parts to each other.

The patriarch of five generations of New Mexico tinsmiths—including his son, Ildeberto "Eddie" Delgado (1883–1966) and granddaughter, Angelina Delgado Martínez—Francisco Delgado sustained the craft of tinwork during the transitional period of the 1920s and 1930s. Angelina Delgado Martínez began making miniature tin pieces for her grandfather in 1931 and has devoted much of her distinguished career to perpetuating tinwork through demonstrations and workshops she has given for the last twenty years.

By the end of the nineteenth century, however, the Industrial Revolution had eliminated the market for many handmade tin objects. Picture frames were mass produced, and oil and gas lighting displaced candle sconces. Individual artisans continued to make pieces in the first two decades of the twentieth century, notably José María Apodaca (1844–1924), known for the scalloped edges and crescent designs on his pieces, and Francisco Sandoval (1860–1944), who opened a tinsmith shop in 1916. Like many tinsmiths, Sandoval was also a roofer, installing the metal roof of the Loretto Chapel in Santa Fe in the 1870s. The majority of the workshops, however, no longer had enough orders to stay in business.

The "revival period" of tinwork in the 1930s, according to Coulter and Dixon, can be attributed to a renewed public interest in traditional Spanish Colonial crafts and to the opening of several commercial outlets in Santa Fe: the Spanish Arts Shop founded by the Spanish Colonial Arts Society in 1930 and the Native Market opened in 1934 by Leonora Curtin:

> Spanish craft stores brought about a shift from a traditionally Hispanic religious patronage to one in which buyers were often tourists, which greatly affected tinwork of the period. The new customers demanded pieces that not only had a "southwestern flavor" but also could be used in modern homes. Frames were made for mirrors instead of religious prints. Most wall sconces, chandeliers, and lanterns were electrified. New forms of tinwork were developed which had not existed in the nineteenth century. Table lamps, flowerpots, tissue holders, and ashtrays were new products of the Revival craftsmen, made in response to the requests of twentieth-century buyers.

Perhaps the most famous of the new shops was the Colonial Tin Antiques Shop, opened in 1929 in Santa Fe by Francisco Delgado (1858–1936) to supplement his income after retirement. A well-educated man with a distinguished career in public service, Delgado had been a tinsmith in his spare time for more than twenty years and had collected examples of nineteenth-century tinwork, which he displayed along with his own pieces at the shop on Canyon Road.

Of equal importance to the new market for tinwork was the surge in popularity of the Pueblo Revival style of architecture, which required regional furniture and appointments. La Fonda Hotel in Santa Fe, for example, had been sold to the Santa Fe Railroad in 1926 to become one of the famous Harvey Houses: it was subsequently furnished with authentic Spanish and Native American crafts, including tin and glass fixtures. Tinwork received further support during the WPA era of national and regional funding for the arts, becoming part of the curriculum at several vocational schools.

To meet the demands of the new tourist market for tin crafts, artisans replaced cast-off tin cans with *terneplate,* sheet iron or steel coated with an alloy of lead and tin. Terneplate was darker in color than tinplate, giving pieces an older, antique quality. Manufactured in West Virginia and used today as well, terneplate is relatively rust-proof and easy to shape, states contemporary tinsmith Angelina Delgado Martínez, and produces crisp seams when soldered. The shift in materials from reclaimed tin cans to sheet metal and the resurgence of public interest in the craft ushered in the modern era of tinwork.

Like many Hispanic artists, Ildeberto Delgado participated in workshops during the WPA era. For this frame (ca. 1937–1938), he collaborated with Eliseo Rodríguez, who did the reverse-painting on glass of the crucifix and the surrounding floral panels. The flowers at the foot of Christ and the angels on either side represent the Resurrection. Delgado made the frame to fit the completed painting by Rodríguez, much as his predecessors might have done for lithographs or painted glass panels in the nineteenth century.

Angelina Delgado Martínez uses many of her father's and grandfather's tools for her work. The birds in this frame are cut from the same template Ildeberto Delgado used in his frame. The designs of the stamp work and embossing are unique to Martínez.

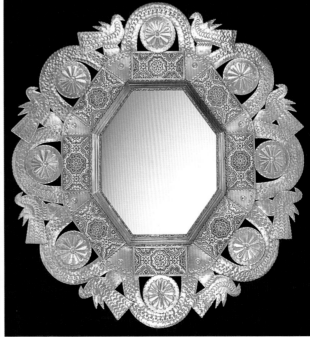

To this nicho, based on nineteenth-century styles, Fred Ray López adds his own innovations of candle holders and twirled brass accents that surround the side panels. Lucy Maestas reverse-painted the glass in the nicho. A grid pattern embellishes the back panel of the nicho. The nicho measures 36 by 35 by 8 inches.

Designs in tinwork were identified in the nineteenth century by the region in which a workshop was located and by the particular styles that emerged from that workshop: for example, Rio Arriba and Rio Abajo styles, the Mora style, Santa Fe Federal, and so on. Many of these styles are models for contemporary artists conscious of working within a historic tradition. The "Mora octagonal" style, for example, produced between 1860 to 1900, is reflected in the tin frame made by Ildeberto Delgado (see page 93). One characteristic of the style is the repeating "C" motif that defines the outside shape of the frame, and the considerable stamp work and embossed designs that cover the surface of the tin. In this frame, the circles attached to the "C" design are embossed with stars, and the birds that adorn the periphery are cut from a single template to make them all uniform. The same "Mora octagonal" design is the prototype for the mirror by Angelina Delgado Martínez. In place of stars on the circles, Martínez has stamped rosettes, and she incorporates brightly colored wallpaper strips instead of reverse-painted glass into the panels circling the edge of the mirror.

The "Valencia red and green" style of 1870–1900 has inspired the double-sided cross by Rita Martínez. The red-and-green painted tin on one side of the cross exemplifies this style, as does the rosette pattern attached to both sides and the single-dot punch design, which is either embossed or flat. The five-petal fleur-de-lis pattern on the base and three corners of the cross represents the Trinity and Mary and Joseph. The small three-petal fleur-de-lis design bisecting the four quadrants of the rosette symbolizes the Trinity.

Elements of the "Rio Arriba" style (1870–1900) characterize Fred Ray López's elaborately constructed nicho; the scalloped edges of the semicircular designs on the sides of the nicho, the rosettes that embellish the arc, and the fan motif on the lunette distinguish this style. Constructed in the shape of a trapezoid, the nicho is further enhanced with reverse painting of roses on glass panels to complement the sacred heart design within the nicho.

This double-sided cross by Rita Valencia Martínez contains strips of handwoven cloth on one side and colcha on the other, both made by Martínez.

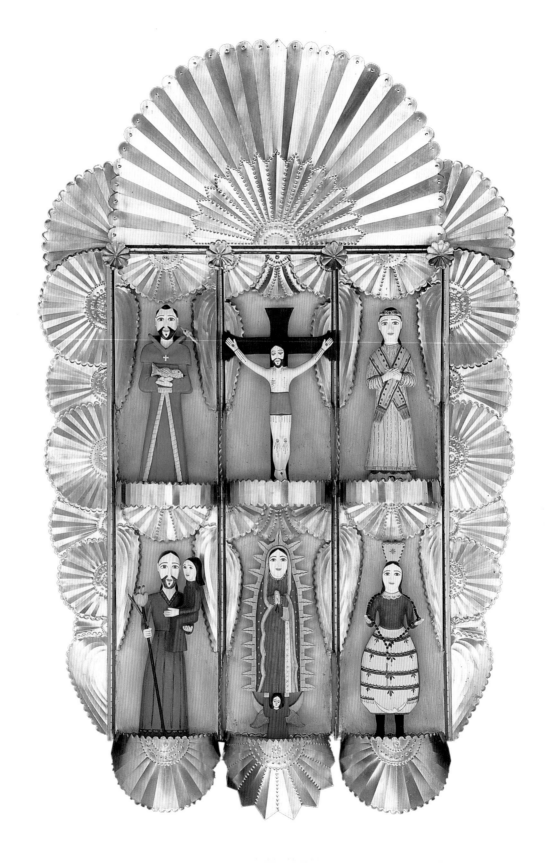

Nichos present contemporary tinsmiths with the greatest opportunity for technical creativity because they are three-dimensional and sculptural. Constructed first as a box or a trapezoid, the majority of nichos have a hinged glass door that closes to protect the santo inside. Glass panels may display colcha-stitch fabric or reverse-painted glass for added decoration. Side columns, a back panel, and the lunette are backdrops for stamp work or embossing. Common stamp designs are rosettes, stars, semicircles, and single dots. Additional embellishments of circles, scrolls, and leaves are frequently attached.

Contemporary artists also experiment with innovative uses of tin. Anita Romero Jones, for example, designs an altar screen in tin with individual nichos to hold her bultos. Tin drapes frame each santo in the classical style of reredoses. The scored lunette on top is embellished with single-dot stamps on each scalloped edge. The columns that would normally frame an altar screen are made of overlapping circle and fan designs, which are further enhanced with stamp work.

The nichos here are all from the personal collections of the artists. Juan D. Martínez's nicho (top left) holds a statue of Santa Rita, for whom he has a special devotion. Jimmy Martin-Madrid's nicho (bottom left) was made to honor the Infant of Prague. Michael Griego has made the *repisa* (wall shelf) on which Robert Duran's Our Lady of Sorrows stands. And Donna Wright de Romero's nicho (bottom right) includes panels of colcha she has embroidered and a St. Isidore carving by Thomas Sena.

Well known for her santero art, Anita Romero Jones made the bultos for this tin altar screen. From the left on the top row are St. Francis, the Crucifixion, and Our Lady of the Immaculate Conception. On the bottom are St. Joseph, Our Lady of Guadalupe, and Our Lady of the Rosary.

This monstrance by Robert Romero has multiple parts. The stand has four individually cut and shaped segments that are soldered to each other. Two frames enclose the retablos. Each ray of the monstrance is individually cut, scored, and soldered to the rest and then to the central vessel. The final composition is cleaned with steel wool and soap and water to remove any acid residue from the soldering that might cause rusting. A final brushing of the tin produces the high sheen. Romero's wife, Annie Romero, assisted him with this piece.

Bonifacio Sandoval began his apprenticeship in tinwork with his uncle, Francisco Sandoval, in 1934 when he was twelve years old. He preserves many of the senior Sandoval's styles in his work.

Another technical tour de force is the *monstrance* by Robert Romero, who is known for his skill in creating complex objects in tin. A monstrance is a framed open or transparent holder in which the consecrated host of the Eucharist is exposed for veneration by the faithful. Romero has placed two miniature retablos of the Crucifixion and Our Lady of Guadalupe painted by Marie Romero Cash in the frame where the host would be shown.

Since the 1930s, contemporary tinsmiths have expanded their repertoire to include utilitarian objects such as elaborate candelabra, wall sconces, and frames for mirrors. Francisco Sandoval is credited with developing the multiple-branched candelabra during the Revival period, similar to those made by his nephew Bonifacio Sandoval. The elongated stem of the center candelabra expresses a modern sensibility in its clean elegant shape, complemented by the circle designs beneath the horizontal branch. The two smaller candelabra are variations on the theme, with the addition of the scroll design anchored by a rosette. Subtle stamp work on the circles and scrolls enhances the overall design.

Robert Romero in his studio, Santa Fe

In the twentieth century, three families stand out for perpetuating the craft of tinwork: the Delgados, the Sandovals, and the Romeros. Trained as a sheet-metal worker, Emilio Romero discovered a natural talent for working with tin, beginning his collaboration with his wife, Senaida, close to fifty years ago. They passed their knowledge and their talent on to their seven children, of whom Robert and Jimmy have become well-known tinsmiths.

Like his father, Robert Romero worked in construction as a sheet-metal worker for nearly thirty years, doing tinwork in his spare time. In 1985, he became a full-time tinsmith. A student of historic pieces, Robert has distinguished himself by recreating historic pieces. He and his sister Marie Romero Cash also popularized the combination of retablos with tin, much as their mother introduced colcha into tin frames. In the tradition of many tinsmithing families, Robert's wife, Annie, collaborates with him on individual pieces, doing some of the punch work, soldering, and finishing work. Their sanctuary lamp hangs above the tabernacle in the Santa María de la Paz Church in Santa Fe.

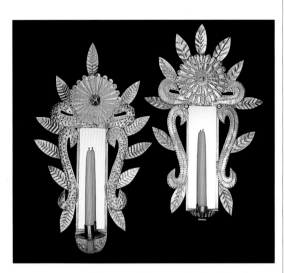

These candle sconces by Emilio and Senaida Romero illustrate methods of decoration. Embossing is a technique of working the back of the tin with a punch so the design stands out on the front side. Stamping is done on the front side of the tin, forming an indentation.

Senaida and Emilio Romero's candle sconces are another example of technical virtuosity in contemporary tinwork. The leaves, rosettes, and scrolls are all individually cut, scored, stamped, and embossed before being assembled. Known for their innovations in design, the Romeros are also recognized for their contribution of combining colcha with tinwork. Despite the long history of colcha embroidery in New Mexico (see chapter 1), the combination of colcha with tin apparently did not exist in nineteenth-century tinwork. Decorative elements instead included wallpaper (sometimes painted with designs), paint on tin, reverse-painted glass, and reverse-painted and combed-glass panels. Colcha patterns in contemporary tinwork are integrated to the overall design of the piece. The finials of the cross by Senaida and Emilio Romero, for example, imitate the floral pattern of the colcha by Senaida.

Versatility is the hallmark of contemporary tinsmiths, who today produce a variety of utilitarian objects—chandeliers, candelabra, lighting fixtures, ornaments, mirrors, frames, and boxes—as well as traditional religious objects, such as crosses, nichos, altar screens, lanterns for *moradas* (meeting houses), and processional crosses. Techniques have changed remarkably little in the one hundred and fifty years since tinwork began in New Mexico: the original cutting shears are now, perhaps, represented by straight cutters and round cutters, but a square and a compass still guide the artist's hand. Punches of various sorts imprint designs, and scoring tools draw the lines for bending the tin, today accomplished with a *bending brake*. A plumber's pipe serves for curving tin into cylindrical shapes, and a soldering iron fixes the parts to each other. Artists make their own stamps and punches but also use the tools passed down by their ancestors. Sheet metal has replaced salvaged cans for the most part, allowing artists greater freedom of expression, but the basic process still requires hours of labor-intensive work.

Entitled *Espejo de Jardín* (Mirror of the Garden), this mirror by Angelina Delgado Martínez exhibits delicate stamp work to reflect the daintiness of the flowers in her colcha embroidery inserts.

Emilio and Senaida Romero have collaborated for over fifty years on their tinwork. Senaida is acknowledged as the first artist to incorporate colcha into tin frames, marking a new direction in the field. This cross measures 34¹/₂ by 20 inches.

Chapter 4

Santero Art

The Chapel of San Ysidro Labrador, Santa Fe

Lorenzo López Sr., the grandfather of contemporary santero Ramón José López, built this chapel (1929–1932) to honor San Ysidro. A santero himself, the elder López carved San Ysidro and his wife, Santa María de la Cabeza, the angel, and many other figures from the story to place on a small altar inside the chapel. Overlooking fields that were still farmed in the 1930s, the *oratorio* was for years a center for community prayers for a good harvest. It fell into disrepair until López (born three years after his grandfather's death) spearheaded a restoration project, completed in 1996. Today, the chapel is owned and maintained by relatives Leopoldo and Andrés Brito. La Capilla de San Ysidro is but one of hundreds of personal chapels built by the Spanish in New Mexico.

ONE OF THE MOST POPULAR SAINTS IN New Mexico is San Ysidro (St. Isidore), the patron saint of farmers. A favorite story about San Ysidro recounts that he was such a good worker (he is also called San Ysidro Labrador, the laborer) that his wife, Santa María de la Cabeza, made him work on a Sunday. God threatened to punish him for working on the Sabbath—first with hail, then with grasshoppers, and finally with a bad neighbor. San Ysidro could not abide the last threat and abandoned his fields to go to mass. While he was at mass, an angel planted his fields, satisfying both God and San Ysidro's wife. In another version of the tale, San Ysidro loved God so much that he spent his days praying in the fields, which God rewarded by sending angels to plow for him.

In New Mexican art, San Ysidro uses the oxdrawn single scratch plow the Spanish colonist would have fashioned roughly out of wood, and he typically wears the broad-brimmed black felt hat, sturdy shoes, and simple clothes of a New Mexican farmer. An angel guides the plow. For generations, Hispanic villagers have celebrated his feast day, May 15th, by carrying an image of San Ysidro through their fields in hopes of a good harvest.

For contemporary *santeros* (those who paint or carve images of saints), San Ysidro is an emblem of the agricultural origins of Spanish New Mexico that bound its inhabitants into tight-knit villages of the faithful. So precious was water, for example, that the colonizers developed a ditch irrigation system, diverting water to individual plots of land from a central ditch, or *acequia madre,* which tapped a stream at its source. Such a system depended upon mutual trust and cooperation among villagers. In his *retablo* (a painting on a flat wooden panel), Belarmino Esquibel dramatizes the deep devotion of San Ysidro by painting him with his head bowed in prayer, oblivious of the angel driving the oxen through the fields.

~ San Yisidro ~

Belarmino
Esquibel

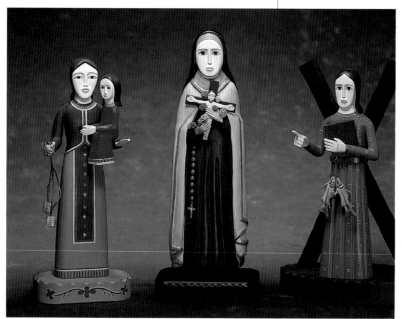

Anita Romero Jones carves St. Andrew against an X-shaped cross, alluding to an early tradition that he was crucified on such a cross. The fish dangling from his belt identify him as a fisherman, the son of John and the brother of Simon Peter. St. Teresa of Ávila, a mystic and Carmelite, is identified by her nun's habit and the crucifix. Our Lady of Carmel is holding the Christ Child, who is traditionally dressed in red.

Page 105
San Ysidro Labrador by Belarmino Esquibel. The rolling hills dotted with piñon and juniper in the background locate the saint in New Mexico. His clothing and wooden spade identify him with a village farmer.

San Ysidro is but one of a pantheon of saints that the Spanish brought with them to the new frontier. Deeply religious, the Spanish settlers clung to their beliefs for solace in the incredibly remote and precarious new world they had entered. Catholicism connected them culturally and socially to Mexico and Spain, from which they were geographically isolated by formidable distances and primitive transportation. Although artwork and other religious objects were imported into the territory from Mexico by caravan every three years during the seventeenth century, the family and ecclesiastical demand for devotional images far exceeded the supply.

The Pueblo Revolt in 1680 essentially destroyed all evidence of the Spanish presence, including their religious artifacts. Soon after the reconquest (1692–1696), Franciscan missionaries, among others, began painting religious subjects on tanned hides of elk, deer, or buffalo to decorate the churches they were rebuilding and to instruct the Pueblo tribes. (Hides had been exported with textiles to Mexico before the revolt.) In the absence of canvas and more conventional painting supplies, hides provided a serviceable material, whether they were acquired at trade fairs from Plains tribes or tanned locally at the Pueblos. Hide painting existed for more than one hundred years until it died out in the nineteenth century due to stylistic changes and a preference for altar screens.

This hide painting by Ramón José López depicts Nuestra Señora de Guadalupe with traditional iconography: the body halo of gold represents the sun's life-giving rays. The crescent moon is an attribute of the Virgin. Guadalupe's brown sash signifies that she will bear a child. The hide itself suggests the cloth of Juan Diego's *tilma*, or cloak. Floral borders frame the narrative painting in the manner of seventeenth-century hide paintings.

Page 102
A detail from an altar screen by Gustavo Victor Goler.

Page 103, top
Our Lady of Sorrows by Gloria López Córdova.

Page 103, bottom
In David Nabor Lucero's *The Coronation of the Virgin Mary by the Holy Trinity*, the figures of the Trinity and the Virgin Mary are carved out of single blocks of sugar pine, with only the hands carved separately out of cottonwood root. The clouds are carved from jelutong, an imported wood that approximates the cottonwood root. The paints are all natural, and the finished bulto is first sealed with pinesap varnish and then with beeswax. Juan D. Martínez made the tin crown of Mary and the halos of the Trinity.

Local *carpinteros* helped the priests rebuild some churches and construct others on new sites, building interior altars, wooden altar screens, and other objects. Some woodworkers eventually became known as santeros because they also provided religious images for the churches. Charles Carrillo, a contemporary santero, notes that the word *santero* did not exist in Spanish Colonial New Mexico: such individuals were called *pintores* (painters), *maestros* (teachers), or *escultores* (sculptors). By the middle of the eighteenth century, local production of santos had become established in response to New Mexico's increased population. With few priests to serve the widely scattered population, villagers sometimes had to wait months for the arrival of a priest to celebrate mass, perform baptisms and marriages, or bless their homes and fields. In the absence of formal church services, settlers built their own personal chapels or dedicated a corner of one room for a home altar, commissioning religious images from local santeros. Santeros also provided bultos, retablos, and reredoses (altar screens containing panels of retablos) for village churches, where colonists might hear mass as infrequently as once a year.

Fray Andrés García, working in New Mexico from 1748 to 1778, made the *Santo Entierro* (a large wooden image of Christ in an open-ribbed casket) for the church at Santa Cruz, which was completed in 1743.

New Mexico's geographical isolation from its cultural home-lands of New Spain, as Mexico was then called, and Spain, and from the United States until the opening of the Santa Fe Trail in 1821, effectively insulated the frontier territory from outside influences for more than two centuries. In his illuminating book on santero art, *Santos and Saints,* Thomas Steele states that "the individualistic point of view which is the hallmark of the Renaissance...eroded almost totally in the isolated colony of New Mexico," which fostered instead collective values of family and community based on a need for mutual protection and survival in a ten-tative agrarian economy. In religious art, the impact of this physical and cultural separation was most pronounced in the santero's departure from classic Renaissance conventions of perspective and realism. Instead, New Mexican santeros evolved a highly individual style that resonates more with medieval painting in its two-dimensionality, stylized facial features, and strong outlines of figures. It was more critical that a santero depict correctly the ecclesiastical attributes of a given saint than render him lifelike.

During the Spanish Colonial (1598–1821) and Mexican Republic (1821–1846) periods, approximately two dozen santeros were responsible for most of the work produced in New Mexico and, of those, few signed their work. Two of the first artists to be identified—Fray Andrés García (a Franciscan from Puebla, Mexico) and Bernardo Miera y Pacheco (a Spanish-born artist, soldier, and cartographer, known for his maps of the Domínguez and Escalante explorations)—were initially commis-sioned to provide images for various churches in the territory. Miera y Pacheco, whose work is distinguished by his use of oils instead of natural pigments and by his adherence to certain conventions of Spanish and Mexican baroque painting, arrived in Santa Fe around 1756. Over the next two decades, he provided images for various Pueblo mission churches, including those at Zuni, Acoma, and San Felipe.

Cristo Crucificado by Alcario Otero shows Christ in the last moment of his Passion. Basing his work upon a similar bulto carved by nineteenth-century santero José Aragón, Otero has added Our Lady of Sorrows and St. John the Apostle as witnesses.

For the next one hundred years (ca. 1750–1850), New Mexico experienced a "golden age" of santero art. Individual artists emerged whose work—and that of their followers—has since been identified by scholars. Pedro Antonio Fresquís, the first identified santero to be born in New Mexico (1749–1831), painted two of the altar screens at the church in Truchas. Molleno—a prolific artist working in New Mexico from ca. 1804 to 1845 and known as the "Chile Painter" for his decorative background motifs—created the large reredos at the Ranchos de Taos church in Taos. José Aragón, in New Mexico from ca. 1820 to 1835, immigrated there from Spain and is the artist of two altar screens in the Santuario de Chimayó. And José Rafael Aragón (ca. 1795–1862), a very popular and productive santero, painted the main altar screen and two smaller screens for the church in Córdova and carved the crucifix for the church in Santa Cruz. Both José Aragón and Rafael Aragón apparently founded and supervised their own workshops to keep up with the demand for their work and are especially known for their bultos. Other santeros, as Robin Gavin states in *Traditional Arts of Spanish New Mexico,* "are referred to by historians according to their styles or some indicative symbol: the 'Laguna Santero' painted the altar screen at the mission church at Laguna Pueblo; the 'A.J. Santero' was named for the initials 'A.J.' that appear on one of his panels; the 'Santo Niño Santero' made numerous images of the Holy Child, and so on."

Although their source of imagery was religious art imported from Mexico, which included prints depicting work by influential European artists, the New Mexican santeros lacked the formal training and materials to reproduce paintings and sculpture in the realistic mode of their Mexican and Spanish counterparts. In place of oil paints, they had mineral and vegetal pigments, which had to be gathered and ground into water-soluble paints. Bultos were fashioned from cottonwood roots and retablo panels were shaped from ponderosa pine trees felled from the forests of northern New Mexico. With few iron tools available, the santero relied on primitive hand adzes and drawknives to smooth wooden panels for retablos and a simple carving knife to carve details into a bulto.

This nineteenth-century bulto of St. Thomas Aquinas by José Rafael Aragón has the elongated and elegant body that is characteristic of Aragón's style and has influenced many contemporary santeros.

111

To prepare retablos and bultos for painting, artisans prepared gesso by mixing native gypsum, which was anhydrated and ground to a flourlike consistency with water and animal glue derived from either boiled hides or hooves. After applying several coats of gesso to the wood and allowing them to dry, the santero then painted the attributes of a given saint. Cochineal and indigo, imported from Mexico for the textile industry, were used sparingly because of their cost. Other colors were formulated from local vegetation and minerals.

So labor intensive was the process of making religious images that santeros considered their work a vocation and were, indeed, deeply religious people. Steele relates that the "tradition of New Mexico santos likewise assumed and demanded that the santero was a holy man, for only thus could the santo be holy and powerful in the religious sphere due both to its maker's holiness and to the holiness of its subject matter." Santos were integral to village and family life and revered for their power to answer prayers and intercede with God on one's behalf.

The santos most often portrayed in the Colonial period exemplify the values of Spanish New Mexico and speak to the harsh reality of life on the frontier. *San Antonio* (St. Anthony), popularly known for his ability to find lost objects and invoked in New Mexico by young women seeking a husband, is also the patron saint of the poor. *Santiago* (St. James the Greater), the patron saint of Spain, is said to have defended Spain against the Moors; in New Mexico, his most famous miracle was at the battle of Acoma in 1599, when he appeared on a white horse to the Indians. After the battle, the Acoma kept asking for the identity of the soldier who had disappeared. *San José* (St. Joseph) represents the family and is variously portrayed either alone holding the infant Jesus or as part of the Holy Family. The flight to Egypt, when the Holy Family escaped from King Herod's infanticide, is a popular tableau in retablos, evocative of the colonists' own journey into a frontier wilderness and of their constant vulnerability to nomadic Indians.

The opening of the Santa Fe Trail in 1821 resulted from Mexico's independence from Spain. By 1826, most Spanish-born priests who did not swear loyalty to Mexico were expelled from New Mexico, replaced by fewer New Mexican and Mexican clergy assigned to the territory. Unlike Spain, which had closed New Mexico to external trade, Mexico opened the borders of its new territory, encouraging free-market capitalism. The Santa Fe Trail became the conduit into New Mexico for both immigrants and a variety of goods, including plaster-cast religious statues and lithographs of religious subjects. The appointment of Jean Baptiste Lamy as the first bishop of New Mexico in 1851 also influenced the future of santero art. Finding many of the adobe churches in serious disrepair, Lamy set about modernizing them with new roofs and church spires that were more in keeping with his European aesthetic. He also changed interiors dramatically by jettisoning the older altar screens and santos, replacing them with mass-produced religious statuary in an attempt to standardize Catholicism in the new territory.

Frank Alarid's bulto of St. Anthony (left), portrayed in the blue robe of his Franciscan order with the Christ Child sitting on his arm, reflects the influence of the Franciscan missionaries in New Mexico. Ernie Luján's St. James (right), the patron saint of soldiers and horses, is depicted on a white horse. Our Lady of Guadalupe, the most revered representation of the Virgin Mary, is by Frank Brito.

In contrast to the official church position on santero art was the growing market for religious images among a lay order of Catholic Hispanic men known as "La Cofradía de Nuestro Padre Jesús Nazareno" or "La Piadosa Fraternidad de Nuestro Padre Jesús Nazareno"—the Penitente Brotherhood. The Penitente Brotherhood emerged during the end of the Colonial period in New Mexico (ca. 1790–1820) in response to the spiritual needs of the growing Hispanic community. In *The Penitentes of the Southwest,* Marta Weigle relates that corruption had become commonplace among the few itinerant priests, who charged "exorbitant fees to perform rites of baptism, confirmation, matrimony, and burial. This deterioration worsened with the population and territorial expansion under Mexican rule."

The Penitente morada in Abiquiú, New Mexico, ca. 1945.

This retablo by Lydia García portrays the Crucifixion of Christ in the upper portion and the fourteen stations of the cross in the lower section. Also called the Way of the Cross, the stations represent separate events in Christ's journey from his condemnation by Pontius Pilate to his descent and burial. The doves symbolize the Resurrection.

José Benjamín López depicts St. Francis of Assisi with Native American features, suggesting the role of the Franciscans among the Pueblo tribes, as well as the contribution of the indigenous peoples to the *mestizo* culture of New Mexico. The saint wears the blue robe worn by Franciscans in New Mexico and displays the stigmata in his hands and sides. The Franciscan cord around his waist symbolizes his servitude to Christ.

El Santo Entierro (Christ in the coffin) by Horacio Valdez. The Penitente crucifix was fashioned with articulated limbs so that Christ could be presented either on the cross with out-stretched arms or within the coffin after death. Also referred to as *Cristo Entierro.*

Into this vacuum of religious leadership stepped the Brothers of Our Father Jesus of Nazarene, who became a particular force for moral and religious order in the northern New Mexico villages. The Penitentes were especially instrumental in sustaining santero art in the nineteenth century because of their devotion to the Passion of Christ—his sufferings between the night of the Last Supper and his death on the cross—which they reenacted with services throughout Holy Week. Indeed, a subcategory of Penitente santero art emerged, in which Christ on the cross was depicted in pitiless detail, from the sacred blood pouring from his wounds to the crown of thorns on his head. In the absence of regular church services, the processions and observances of the Penitentes filled a void in village life, paralleling the sacraments of the Catholic mass.

Every *morada* (meeting house) contained an altar with santos revered
by its membership. St. Francis of Assisi (1181–1226), the founder of the
Franciscans, for example, was popular among some of the Penitentes,
who identified with the saint's dedication to the poor and sick of the
world despite his birth to privilege and wealth. They also revered his
devotion to the suffering of Christ, made manifest by his receiving
the stigmata. In their bultos and retablos, santeros portrayed St. Francis
with stigmata and sometimes a skull—symbols of salvation and mortality.

Mi Comadre Sebastiana— Emperatriz de Muerte (My godmother Sebastiana— empress of death) by Charles Carrillo. Of the bow and arrow, Carrillo, a member of the Abiquiú morada, writes: "In Colonial New Mexico, specifically in 1824, at the beginning of the Mexican Republic period, the Urban Militia of New Mexico was armed with bow and arrows...made by the Hispanic men in the militia...the tips or arrowpoints were made of *pedernal* or obsidian. The tradition of handmade flint, or obsidian-tipped arrows, is very much a Hispanic tradition. The preparation and use of obsidian blades still exists among the Penitente Brotherhood in New Mexico."

A death cart by Horacio Valdez. In some instances, Doña Sebastiana's *carreta* was filled with rocks and pulled through the streets during Holy Week as an act of penance, as well as a potent symbol of man's mortality.

The *carreta de muerte,* or "death cart," was another ubiquitous fixture in the moradas of Los Hermanos. In New Mexico, *La Muerte,* the image of death, is represented by a female skeleton known as Doña Sebastiana. In *Images of Penance, Images of Mercy,* William Wroth states that the origins of the death cart most probably go back to the "procession of the Descent and Burial of Christ, signifying His victory over death." Shrouded in black, Doña Sebastiana is typically portrayed as an old hag, holding a bow and arrow, waiting to shoot her next victim. Wroth speculates that the bow and arrow probably refers to St. Sebastian, who was ordered executed by bow and arrow in the third century. Doña Sebastiana and the death cart are the only examples of nineteenth-century santero art that were not replaced by mass-produced images. Santeros continued to make the carretas de muerte upon request for local chapters of the Brotherhood.

The Brotherhood's ritual acts of penance—including self-flagellation and carrying *maderos* (heavy wooden crosses) during Easter Week processions to dramatize Christ's journey to Calvary—inevitably came into direct conflict with the official church, forcing the Penitentes to become private and clandestine for a number of years. Ironically, in their retreat behind the walls of their moradas, they preserved much of the santero art that the church wished to discard or replace with mass-produced images. Further, as more Protestant sects entered the New Mexico territory under the American occupation after 1846, the Penitente Brotherhood became more committed to preserving the material art of their Catholic faith that had sustained their ancestors for more than two centuries.

Nevertheless, by the end of the nineteenth century, the demand for retablos and bultos had declined dramatically because of the availability of mass-produced religious imagery, which, perhaps, appealed to New Mexicans because of its newness. José Benito Ortega (1858–1941) was the last major santero of the nineteenth century, working until 1907. Itinerant santeros filled orders in rural villages from time to time, but the slow decline in santero art would not be reversed until the second decade of the twentieth century, when Anglo art patrons Mary Austin and Frank Applegate would first investigate the work of Celso Gallegos in Agua Fria and then "discover" the work of José Dolores López during their excursions to Córdova to view the Holy Week processions.

Bulto of Our Lady of Solitude by José Benito Ortega. Thomas Steele describes this representation of the Virgin Mary in *Santos and Saints:* "Between her son's crucifixion and resurrection and between his ascension and her own death, Mary lived (according to Christian folklore) like a nun...Mary is dressed in a very nun-like black and white...she rarely holds anything in her hands, but bultos of La Soledad are often designed with arms that can hold a towel on which the implements of the passion...are placed."

In the first two decades of the twentieth century, New Mexico became a mecca for eastern artists and writers attracted to the region's breathtaking landscapes and distinctive Pueblo and Hispanic cultures. This was the era of the Taos Society of Artists, founded in 1915. The Museum of Fine Arts was founded in Santa Fe in 1917. In 1921, "Los Cinco Pintores," a group of five Santa Fe artists, began to organize exhibitions of their work to distinguish themselves from the already established Santa Fe Artists Club organized in 1920. And in 1925, the Spanish Colonial Arts Society was created to preserve and perpetuate traditional Hispanic arts. Travel to the northern New Mexico villages became easier with the automobile in the 1920s, increasing opportunities for patrons to meet artists, which in turn revived the market for handmade objects.

Such a patronage relationship developed between Mary Austin and Frank Applegate, founding members of the Spanish Colonial Arts Society, and José Dolores López (1868–1937), a wood-carver from Córdova. The son of a santero, Nasario López, José Delores pursued carpentry as a trade for many years, although he was intimately familiar with santero art through his membership in the Córdova morada of the Penitente Brotherhood, serving as *hermano mayor,* or leader, at one point. He did not, however, take up wood carving as an avocation until 1917, when his oldest son was drafted into World War I. Deeply anxious over the possibility of losing his son, López turned to carving to occupy his mind. When his son safely returned in 1919, López had become captivated by his recent therapy, making gifts for friends and pieces for the town chapel and the morada.

Our Lady of Light bulto by José Dolores López illustrates the complexity of his chip-carving and his talent for perspective and assemblage. There are twenty-eight separate rays in Mary's halo that frame the centerpiece of her crown, all of which have been individually carved and decorated before being placed in the crown itself, which is then attached to the torso of the bulto, as are the arms.

George López, Córdova, New Mexico. By 1960, George López had distinguished himself as the first Córdova wood-carver to earn a living from his art. His wife, Silvianita, collaborated with him, performing the painstaking task of *laboreando la cosa*, or chip-carving designs on each bulto with a penknife. It is not unusual for couples or family members to work together on pieces, though generally only one person signs the finished carving.

The middle bulto of St. Francis is by Leonard Salazar. The other bultos of St. Francis (left) and St. Joseph (right) are by his father, Leo Salazar. The variegated colors of cedar—red, gray, and white— are characteristic of the work of Leo Salazar, who used the colors to delineate different aspects of the dress or to suggest movement in the bultos. The white crosses and the white bird are carved from aspen wood.

With the support of Applegate and other Anglo collectors, López found a new market for his work that would also change the direction of his carving. His earlier furniture pieces had been painted in bright, garish house paints, which Applegate persuaded him to abandon in favor of leaving the wood unpainted. To decorate the surfaces of his pieces, López developed a chip-carving technique of chiseling out intricate patterns in the wood, similar to the ornamental openwork of filigree jewelry he had made earlier in his career. Applegate also influenced López to turn his talents to carving religious figures, which he did for only a brief decade before his death in 1937. Nonetheless, his bultos produced between 1927 and 1937 launched a new direction in santero art, away from the painted images of the historic santeros to the unpainted, carved style that is still characteristic of Córdova wood carving today.

López's most famous pupil turned out to be his son, George López (1900–1993), who took up carving in 1925 and returned to it full-time in 1952 upon retirement from his job at Los Alamos National Laboratory. Like many artisans from the northern New Mexico villages, López had to seek employment away from home to support his family. Charles Briggs says in *The Wood Carvers of Córdova, New Mexico* that the transition in village life after New Mexico became a state in 1912 was pronounced for Hispanic people, because the American economic system was "predicated upon the replacement of handmade goods with mass-produced goods and the conversion of self-sufficient farmers and ranchers into dependent wage earners." Communal grazing lands, which had once sustained small herds of livestock owned by villagers, had been subsumed into national forests around 1900 or were turned over to large cattle ranchers, severely limiting the Hispanic's ability to be economically self-sufficient. By 1915, many Hispanics were forced to seek employment on the railroad, as migrant laborers or ranch hands, or in urban centers far removed from their homes. George López himself had worked in sheep camps and as a fruit picker.

The Last Supper by Patrocinio Barela.
Barela's influence on contemporary santeros has been profound, as Luis Tapia
affirms: "Freedom is probably the most
important aspect of his work to me.
And his having the courage to take his
art his own way, especially when he had
to battle poverty all the time."

Contemporary with José Dolores López was another wood-carver, Patrocinio Barela (1908–1964) from Taos, who has also influenced contemporary santeros. A deeply spiritual man with no formal education, Barela was a completely self-taught artist, who carved in a surrealistic modern style, reminiscent of cubism. Like other Hispanic artists during the depression, Barela was employed by the WPA Federal Art Project to produce art for government institutions. In 1936, Barela was one of 171 artists out of thousands in the program selected to show his work at the Museum of Modern Art in New York, and he immediately became the most celebrated artist in the show, receiving national attention.

Barela constantly explored the condition of man in his sculpture, depicting sacred and secular subjects in homuncular shapes. He carved santos and religious stories in relief work and sculptures of unpainted pine, cedar, and juniper, following the natural formations of the wood itself. His organic style departed dramatically from the work of other santeros. Barela's most immediate successor was Leo Salazar (1933–1991), who apprenticed with him in the late 1960s and became distinguished for his unpainted carvings of religious figures. Using cedar wood gathered from the forests near Taos, Salazar developed a technique of following the grain of the wood and allowing a figure to emerge, carving in details of the face and posture of the saint, but leaving the body to follow the shape of the wood (see page 123).

In quite distinct ways, both José Dolores López and Patrocinio Barela struck out in new directions that redefined tradition in twentieth century santero art. López moved away from the painted bultos of the eighteenth- and nineteenth-century santeros to create intricate wood carvings in unpainted wood that exemplify the Córdova style of today. And Barela, in pursuing his own vision apart from the mainstream, became a model for a generation of Hispanic artists, who would come into their own in the decades after his death.

§

Ben Ortega in his studio

Renowned for his carvings of St. Francis in natural wood, Ben Ortega portrays the saint's joy in the miracle of nature with birds on his shoulder. Ortega gathers his own wood and finds the shape of his images in the natural grain of the wood. He carved a large St. Francis for the Monastery of Christ in the Desert near Abiquiú.

Charles Carrillo in his studio, Santa Fe

For Charles Carrillo, hand-adzing a piece of pine for a retablo, preparing homemade gesso, or grinding his own pigments for painting is as critical to the artistic process as his final product. A scholar of Spanish Colonial art and history —he has a doctorate in anthropology and did his dissertation on Spanish Colonial New Mexican Hispanic pottery—Carrillo is credited as one of a handful of santeros who reintroduced the original pigments of the seventeenth, eighteenth, and nineteenth centuries into contemporary santero art. (The other santeros include Félix López, Ramón José López, and members of La Escuelita.) Through researching historical documents, including dyes and mordants related to Spanish Colonial weaving, and experimenting with natural minerals and plants, Carrillo has reproduced the natural colors of the historic santeros that have, he says, "a vibrancy and a softness to them."

A born educator, Carrillo is generous with his research and has become the mentor and teacher for a group of santeros, informally known as La Gavilla (The gang), who gather periodically at Carrillo's home to carve or paint together or just to share ideas. Members include Jerome and Ernie Luján, Arlene Cisneros Sena, David Nabor Lucero, Jimmy and Debbie Trujillo, Alcario Otero, Debbie Carrillo, Charlie Sánchez, Nicholas Herrera, José Armijo, Raymond López, and others. In the tradition of La Escuelita and La Cofradía, La Gavilla mounts exhibits of contemporary santero art in private homes and community centers.

A member of the Abiquiú morada, Carrillo sees santero art as a way of honoring tradition and community. "This is the first time in our history that we have a pen in our hands. We can begin to write our own history. These santos, these colors, this tradition tells our history."

In 1965, E. Boyd, the renowned curator for the Museum of New Mexico who resurrected the Spanish Colonial Arts Society in 1952, revived the society's annual Spanish Market in Santa Fe, which had been defunct since Mary Austin's death in 1934. That same year, President Lyndon Johnson signed the Voting Rights Act, one year after he had signed the historic Civil Rights Act into law. In New Mexico, the "Civil Rights Movement," states Charles Carrillo, "woke up the consciousness of the land grant activists. It gave people a voice and made people aware of their roots. From that comes art. The Movement empowered people to have a voice that counts, and to embrace art forms that are ancestral, art that belongs to them." This consciousness expressed itself in a flowering of santero art, which Carrillo says, "never died out [in the twentieth century]. Santero art just died back."

With heightened pride in their ancestry, artists organized grassroots groups in the Spanish tradition of *talleres* (workshops). Santero José Benjamín López and his wife, Irene, a weaver, were instrumental in bringing together a group of wood-carvers from Española in the early 1970s, who met regularly at their homes to carve together and exchange information on technique, history, aesthetics, and philosophy. Known informally as "La Escuelita" (the little school), they mounted an unprecedented exhibition of contemporary and traditional Hispanic art in 1978, bringing public attention to the resurgence in religious art occurring among Hispanic artists.

Another organization, "La Cofradía de Artes y Artesanos Hispánicos" (Brotherhood of Hispanic Arts and Artisans), was also founded in the 1970s by artists Luis Tapia and Frederico Vigil to renew interest in traditional art forms and provide a new venue for showing Hispanic art, which was not supported by mainstream art galleries at the time. Tapia recalls La Cofradía's first exhibition at the Santuario de Guadalupe in Santa Fe in 1979: "There were over three hundred artists in that show. The suppression of our art was overwhelming when you realized how many artists were working out there." Over the next few years, La Cofradía organized exhibitions at churches, community centers, universities, and museums before officially disbanding in 1983. By then, however, they had more than fulfilled their goal of bringing Hispanic art into the public arena.

By the mid-1970s, there were more than six times the number of new santeros entering the field than had worked during the entire Spanish Colonial era. Thomas Steele has called the contemporary period a "Romantic Revival," noting that "revival" santeros are likely to be familiar with artistic traditions other than their own, and that they often learn their art through their own research or mentoring with other santeros. They market their work to collectors and sign their pieces as artists. They include women (santeras have yet to be identified in the historic period). And they occasionally enter special relationships with advisor/patrons, who in turn can influence the direction of their art (such as the patronage between José Dolores López and Frank Applegate).

St. Michael by La Escuelita member Luisito Luján. Membership in La Escuelita has included Olivar Martínez, Clyde Salazar, Leroy López, José Alberto Baros, Félix López, Manuel López, Olivar Rivera, Tim Roybal, and José Griego. In existence for over twenty years now, La Escuelita continues to meet when families and jobs permit.

Contemporary santero art can be divided into two categories: flat art (retablos and altar screens) and three-dimensional art (bultos). Retablos evolved historically in the absence of canvas for paintings. Like their forebears, contemporary artists use pine, which they cut into any number of shapes, including rectangles, squares, ovals, and circles for retablos. (Historic santeros generally carved only rectangular shapes for retablos.) Some artists work from scratch, hand-adzing the wood and shaving off a portion of the back of the piece so it will hang flat against the wall from a leather thong. Others use milled lumber. After cutting the wood to the desired shape, the santero applies several coats of gesso, which is sanded after it dries to provide a smooth surface for painting. Paints may be water-based or oil-based, commercial or home-made from vegetal and mineral sources.

Retablos by Arlene Cisneros Sena. The top row from the left includes Nuestra Señora de Guadalupe, San José, and Santa Verónica. On the bottom row from the left are San Pascual, Santa Librada, and La Sagrada Familia. An admirer of the eighteenth-century santero Bernardo Miera y Pacheco, Sena emulates his classic style in the delicate faces of her saints and the elegant draping of their clothing. Like Miera y Pacheco, Sena originally painted in oils but has since switched to natural pigments, deriving ochre from oxide-based minerals, brown from micaceous clay, black from black walnut hulls, and yellow from chamisa. She mixes black walnut hulls with indigo to get a gray wash, and she also uses 23-karat gold leaf.

Subjects for retablos are usually individual saints, who are invoked for their power to address temporal, as well as spiritual, problems. Popular saints in New Mexico include Santa Bárbara, who protects one from lightning, and Santa Lucía, who defends against blindness. San Ysidro is petitioned for a good harvest. San José protects the family, and San Antonio helps find lost objects. San Acacio, a legendary saint, defends against enemy forces, and San Francisco de Asís—patron saint of Santa Fe—answers virtually all prayers.

San Pascual has become ubiquitous as the patron saint of the kitchen and is usually portrayed in a New Mexico kitchen with a beehive oven and chiles in the background. Charles Carrillo relates that San Pascual was, in fact, the patron saint of shepherds. Also a Franciscan missionary, he was assigned to make the bread for the Eucharist. So great was the saint's devotion to the Eucharist that it appeared to him in a monstrance, the vessel in which the consecrated host is held before the people. San José is also especially appealing to New Mexicans, notes Carrillo, because he was a carpenter and, as the husband of Mary, he provided Christ with a home.

Retablos may be embellished with a lunette (half-moon shell design) on the top of the panel, such as those of San Pascual, San José, and the Holy Family by Arlene Cisneros Sena. The saints themselves are often bordered by curtains, as in Sena's retablo of Saint Veronica. According to Roland Dickey in *New Mexico Village Arts,* this "convention derived from the draperies put on saints' niches so the figures could be shrouded during Holy Week."

Nicholas Herrera in his one-hundred-year-old studio, El Rito

Nicholas Herrera grew up next to his grandfather's house in El Rito, which he remodeled years later into this studio, where he works on his retablos and bultos and constructions that have earned him a national reputation as an "outsider artist." He depicts Doña Sebastiana, for example, riding a motorcycle instead of a wooden carreta, and he paints the traditional santos with a unique unself-conscious imagination that categorizes him as a true folk artist.

Keenly aware of the legacy of the historic santeros—his great uncle José Inez Herrera was a santero known as the El Rito Santero of Death—Herrera nevertheless has pursued his own vision in his art. Like many santeros, Herrera's avocation of making religious art became a true vocation when he suffered a personal disaster. Almost dying from an automobile accident, Herrera had a vision of death while he was in a coma—a figure of La Muerte his uncle had made. After his recovery, Herrera made the decision to dedicate himself to his art, which he describes as "social commentary in the contemporary world. My roots are tradition, and I put tradition next to what's going on in today's world."

Frames are another area for decoration, as Sena has done in the retablo of Guadalupe, adding roses as an emblem of the Virgin's miraculous appearance to Juan Diego. Ramón José López frames his retablos of Adam and Eve and San Camilo de Lelis in sterling silver boxes, which serve as reliquaries for rosaries or other religious objects. The patron saint of nurses, San Camilo de Lelis ministers to a Native American, locating him in New Mexico.

Altar screens are large wooden panels of individually painted sections, bordered by columns and installed behind the altar of a church. Some altar screens include a nicho for a central figure, usually the patron saint of a community or the Crucifixion. The pattern of an altar screen includes horizontal rows of two or three sections each in which saints are painted as they would be in retablos. The larger scale allows for more background detail and figurative motifs in the draperies and frames. An image of God the Father or the Trinity is often painted above the figures, and a lunette design may adorn the top of the altar screen. Side columns are sometimes elaborately carved in a style reminiscent of baroque art, while others are flat and only serve to frame the panels. Floral designs often complete the composition.

These handmade sterling silver boxes by Ramón José López have a thin layer of transparent mica that covers the surface of each retablo, adding another dimension to the paintings. Before glass panes were introduced into New Mexico, selenite glazing was used in church windows so they could admit natural light.

Gustavo Victor Goler carved this altar screen from pine and prepared it with homemade gesso before painting the images. The paints are watercolors, which are sealed with piñon sap varnish. Trained as a conservationist, Goler worked with santeros Félix López, Manuel López, and José Benjamín López for a year, conserving the nineteenth-century altar screen by José Rafael Aragón at the Holy Cross Church in Santa Cruz de la Cañada.

Of her altar screen, Mónica Sosaya Halford says, "I paint the saints I'm closest to. I always try to keep the Holy Family together in my altar screens [that is, St. Joseph is painted next to the Virgin and Child]. St. Francis is the patron saint of Santa Fe, and he and San Antonio are favorites of mine."

Altar screens are also made for home altars and family chapels, which remain as ubiquitous in the twentieth century as they were in the Spanish Colonial era. Gustavo Victor Goler's altar screen (see page 131) incorporates conventions of Mexican baroque art in the twisted columns with decorative scrolls on either side. Shell patterns border the central lunette, under which an angel is painted. The three saints on the top row stand on tiles, another Mexican influence, while the angels on the bottom row hover upon clouds. From left to right on the top row, St. Teresa is portrayed with a feather pen, signifying her role as a writer, and the small edifice in the background represents the many convents she founded in sixteenth-century Spain. The center figure is St. Joseph, and on the right is St. Barbara, who was first imprisoned and then killed by her father for refusing to marry because of her faith. He in turn was struck dead by lightning. The three windows in the tower represent the Trinity and are an emblem of St. Barbara's deep devotion. On the bottom row, the Immaculate Conception—an advocation of the Virgin Mary emphasizing her freedom from Original Sin—is bordered by the Guardian Angel on the left and San Rafael on the right.

Mónica Sosaya Halford's altar screen includes angels at the top of the pillars on either side of God the Father. Two doves are painted at the bottom of the columns, ascending toward God, whose hand is raised in a blessing. In the other hand, He holds a thunderbolt, symbolizing His omnipotence. The sun and moon on either side of God represent the Creation. The first row of saints (from left to right) includes San José, Our Lady of Refuge holding the Christ child, and the Santo Niño de Atocha. On the second row are St. Francis holding a skull, San Felipe de Neri (before a church of the same name in Albuquerque), and San Antonio.

This chapel, inspired by Zoraida Ortega's devotion to Our Lady of Guadalupe, was built by Zoraida and Eulogio Ortega in 1980–1982 for their own private worship after their retirement from teaching (he was an elementary school principal, and she taught art and bilingual education in elementary school). Their altar screen, which Eulogio built of pine and Zoraida painted—it took her a year to complete it—consists of a central nicho for the crucifix, above which is a dove, the symbol for the Holy Spirit. To the popular New Mexico santos of San Ysidro, San Rafael, and San José to the left of the crucifix, the Ortegas added Our Lady of La Joya, since Velarde was originally named La Joya. To the right of the crucifix are images of Our Lady of Sorrows, the Santo Niño de Atocha, Nuestra Señora de Guadalupe, and San Antonio. Eulogio carved the crucifix and the bultos of Our Lady of Guadalupe, San Rafael, and San Ysidro. Zoraida painted all of the bultos and designed and painted all of the decorative motifs on the columns. The entire project took five years to complete. Two historic santos appear on either side of the altar screen: Our Lady of Solitude (right) by José Benito Ortega, and San José (left) by an anonymous santero.

Of their work of art, built out of love and devotion, Eulogio says, "The chapel has transformed our lives by bringing visitors from every European country, Central America, Mexico, and almost every state of the Union. Everything else is of small consequence. I consider the rest of our activity as an afterthought really." The Ortegas have also carved and painted crucifixes to donate to a number of churches in northern New Mexico and completed commissions for various museums.

The interior of Our Lady of Guadalupe Chapel, Velarde

Marie Romero Cash has based her altar screen on one of the side altars painted by José Aragón in 1820 for the Santuario de Chimayó. God the Father watches over three advocations of the Virgin Mary: Our Lady of Carmel, the Immaculate Conception, and Our Lady of St. John of the Lakes in the top row. St. Francis, St. Jerome, and St. Anthony compose the second row. And the angels Gabriel and Michael flank the sacred heart cross on the bottom row.

In contrast to the altar screens of Goler, Halford, and Cash is Luis Tapia's *Dashboard Altar.* Brightly painted with acrylics and original in concept, the altar is Tapia's interpretation of the importance of cars and Catholicism in New Mexican Hispanic culture. A guardian angel hovers above the dashboard, on which two saints stand. Doña Sebastiana, the figure of death, sits in the back seat and is visible through the rearview mirror—a somber reminder of highway deaths. On the steering wheel is the Sacred Heart of Jesus, revered by the faithful and petitioned for forgiveness of sins. Through the front window stretches the solitary New Mexico landscape.

§ § §

**Marie Romero Cash in her
studio, Santa Fe**

In 1996, Marie Romero Cash was commissioned by the archdiocese of Santa Fe to paint the fourteen stations of the cross for St. Francis Cathedral in Santa Fe, becoming the first Hispanic artist to contribute santero art to the predominantly French-Romanesque church. This project is the latest in a long line of prestigious commissions Romero Cash has garnered: she has painted altar screens for churches in El Rito, Arroyo Hondo, Santa Fe, Ojo Caliente, Española, and Albuquerque, as well as for churches in Pueblo and San Luis, Colorado. In preparing for her first commission, Romero Cash visited all of the churches in northern New Mexico to study the altar screens of the historic santeros. Realizing that no one had done an inventory of the art in the churches, she embarked on a three-year research project that culminated in her book, *Built of Earth and Song— Churches of Northern New Mexico.*

Romero Cash began carving bultos and painting retablos in the mid-1970s. The daughter of renowned tinsmiths Emilio and Senaida Romero, she grew up surrounded by traditional New Mexican art. Her sister, Anita Romero Jones, is a santera, and two of her brothers, Robert Romero and Jimmy Romero, are tinsmiths. While she is a meticulous student of historic santero art, Romero Cash is also an innovative artist, known for her unique interpretations of religious art: Adam and Eve in a carousel; Our Lady of the Harvest, a distinctive interpretation of the Virgin Mary; and a chess set in which all the players are santos (the knights are bultos of St. James, the queen is the Virgin Mary, the king is San José, and the pawns are Hispanic soldiers from 1860).

Of the inspiration to make dashboard altars, Luis Tapia recalls, "My mother's car was a real dashboard altar. She had a 1957 Chevy, and she always hung a rosary from the rearview mirror and had plastic figures of Jesus and Mary on the dashboard. This is another expression of the influence of Catholicism in our culture."

Marie Romero Cash has painted a kneeling St. Jerome in her altar screen (the middle figure of the middle row) with his traditional attributions of a beard and red cloak. The trumpet symbolizes the voice of God. St. Jerome (344–420) is renowned for his translation of the Bible from Hebrew and Greek into the Latin Vulgate version, the standard until 1979.

Eurgencio López carving outside his home in Córdova

Like his grandfather José Dolores López and his uncle George López, Eurgencio López uses the native woods of northern New Mexico—aspen, pine, juniper, and willow—for his carvings. Most of these woods have to be cut by the early summer so the bark can be stripped and the wood dried. The head, torso, and feet are commonly shaped out of a single block of wood, and the arms, crowns, or other accouterments are carved out of separate pieces of wood and then attached to the torso with glue. The more elaborate compositions sometimes require dozens of individually carved pieces, all of which are first sanded to a smooth finish before being incised with chip-carving. The final step includes assembling the pieces with glue and then sanding them one final time to eliminate rough edges or seams.

For much of the twentieth century, bultos remained unpainted after the style of José Dolores López, whose influence remains strong among his descendants and other contemporary wood-carvers of Córdova. The Córdova style is characterized by chip-carving, which, in the absence of paints, delineates facial features and aspects of dress, as well as decorating the bases upon which santos are placed. Briggs notes that "on a well-carved piece only the chip-carving remains to demonstrate clearly that the work was in fact carved. This separates the Córdovan wood-carving style from many modern . . . sculptures."

Gloria López Córdova, a granddaughter of José Dolores López, has developed her own style of chip carving, which is deep and precise. In Our Lady of Sorrows, she embroiders the base of the bulto with diamond and rosette motifs. The dress of Our Lady is covered with ornate designs, and the rays of the halo are individually carved. Córdova conveys the anguish of Mary, who grasps the sword plunged into her heart—a symbol of her deep mourning over the Crucifixion of Christ.

Sabinita López Ortiz, also a granddaughter of José Dolores López, learned to carve from George López. Unable to have children, George and Silvianita López adopted Sabinita (one of five children of George's brother Ricardo) as an infant. Both Córdova and Ortiz combine aspen wood with cedar in their bultos. Córdova uses the darker cedar wood in the halo of Our Lady of Sorrows and for the wings of the angel. In her bultos (see page 145), Ortiz outlines the veil of Our Lady of the Rosary (center figure) with cedar, using her chip-carving to delicately decorate the clothing and bases of the bultos. The Blessed Mother and St. Michael the Archangel flank Our Lady of the Rosary.

Our Lady of Sorrows by Gloria López Córdova. This image of the Virgin Mary suffering grief over Christ's Crucifixion struck a particular chord with the Spanish colonists as an emblem of the hardships they endured.

The Temptation of Saint Anthony by Luis Tapia. Devils and a serpent attempt to lure St. Anthony to the temptations of alcohol and the carnal life, while the figure of Death looms overhead, ready to take both his spirit and his body.

While the Córdova woodworkers primarily carve unpainted bultos, the majority of contemporary santeros have returned to making polychrome bultos over the last twenty years (as did the historic santeros), following the lead of santeros Orlando Romero, Luis Tapia, and Horacio Valdez, who reintroduced painted bultos to Spanish Market in the 1970s. Prior to founding La Cofradía, Tapia had studied collections of religious art at the Museum of International Folk Art and visited village churches to study how the old santos had been made. Beneath layers of age and dust, Tapia discovered bright colors, which had softened with age. Convinced that the historic santeros painted their bultos with primary colors, Tapia incorporated a vivid palette into his own work, opening the door for new interpretations of traditional subjects as illustrated in the *Dashboard Altar* and *The Temptation of Saint Anthony*.

During the same period, Horacio Valdez (1929–1992), a santero from Dixon, had found his vocation in carving and painting santos. A carpenter by trade, Valdez turned to carving when an accident prevented him from working for months. Like José Dolores López, Valdez found that carving was more than just a way to pass the time: it was a calling. Deeply religious—he became a member of the Penitente Brotherhood, as had his father and his grandfather—Valdez became a master carver, known for his penitential art. He also made over two hundred crucifixes, one of which was given to Pope John Paul II. Completely self-taught, Valdez used rich acrylic paints on his bultos, an innovation at the time, that has since influenced a new generation of santeros.

Since the mid-1970s, the number of contemporary santeros who make painted bultos has grown dramatically, in part as a conscious revival of historic styles but also because painted santos offer the greatest opportunities for artists to express their individual talents. The subjects for bultos, noted by Steele, include "the divine persons—God the Father, Christ, and the Holy Spirit . . . Mary according to various titles or advocations . . . the angels . . . the male and female saints . . . and the impersonal and allegorical subjects."

Nicholas Herrera, for example, interprets the Trinity as three attached torsos, bound together by a crown of thorns, symbolizing the suffering of Jesus Christ. A dove, the emblem for the Holy Spirit, looks down from above. The three identical bearded young men of the Trinity are portrayed as Christ—a convention, states Carrillo, of humanizing God and moving away from the angry Yahweh of the Old Testament that grew out of the sixteenth-century Reformation in Europe. In some interpretations, the three figures of the Trinity hold a lightning bolt to represent their divine omnipotence.

The Trinity by Nicholas Herrera. The three crosses on top of the altar are similar to those that dot the New Mexico landscape, marking the *descansos*, or resting places, of the pallbearers on the way to the *campo santo* (cemetery).

Félix López at his studio, Española

A santero for more than twenty-five years, Félix López has quietly pioneered new directions in the field of religious art. Known for his bultos, carved and gessoed and painted with traditional methods, López nevertheless adds his own unique stamp to each piece by depicting the attributes of the saints in new ways: for example, in portraying St. Francis, he might place the skull, traditionally held in the saint's hand, behind his foot instead. His most recent bultos have Spanish inscriptions written on the bottom of the bases, which reflect the special thoughts or prayers that come to mind while he is making a piece. López also strives to make his multifigured bultos dynamic rather than static, inclining the figures toward each other to suggest motion and the relationships that exist in the story he is portraying. He says, "I'm trying to learn more from the santos, to let them be my spiritual teachers and to enrich my life."

La Coronación de la Virgen María por la Santísima Trinidad by David Nabor Lucero also represents the Trinity as three distinct but identical bearded young men (see page 103). They are holding a rope that symbolizes their unity, and their triangular halos further reinforce the theme of Three-in-One. God is about to crown the Virgin Mary, symbolizing her central role as Mother of Christ. Floating on ethereal clouds, the Trinity is beyond time and space, the ultimate mystery of Christianity.

Christ as a young child, another popular subject for santeros within the category of divine personages, is variously carved as the Santo Niño de Atocha (see introduction); the Niño Perdido (Lost Child, referring to when Christ stayed behind at the temple at age twelve), the Santo Niño (Divine Child), and as the Niño de Praga (Infant of Prague). In Charles Carrillo's *Santo Niño Flor de María* (Infant Child, Flower of Mary), the Christ Child is enthroned upon a lily, the symbol of purity and a reference to the Immaculate Conception. The Christ Child is holding a blue orb with a cross on top, representing his dominion over the world. The two candles on either side are inscribed with Latin indulgences.

While contemporary santeros base their retablos, bultos, and reredoses on traditional religious subject matter, they are also innovative in their artistic interpretations. *Jesus Cures the Blind Man* by Félix López marks a new direction in santero art (see page 142). In place of the single-figure bultos, López has created a sculptural narrative of four bultos. An admirer of nineteenth-century santero José Rafael Aragón, López elongates the bodies of his figures in the style of Aragón but goes beyond Aragón in the gracefulness of his carving and the molding of his gesso to make the figures dynamic rather than static, engaged in a sculptural dialogue with each other. His palette of rich colors derives from natural pigments.

Inspired by a sermon on the miracles of Christ, Félix López selected the story of "Jesus Cures the Blind Man" for this multifigured bulto. Christ reaches out his right hand and places it over the blind man's head. Looking at him, and with his left hand raised in prayer, Jesus makes the man see again. Next to Jesus are two of his disciples, who have been accompanying him and at this moment are witnessing the miracle.

Gustavo Victor Goler captures the spiritual drama of the miracle of Nuestra Señora de Guadalupe by framing the Virgin on a celestial stage. All of the conventions of retablo art—the lunette and scrolls, floral motifs, and painted columns—are the stage set for this singular story.

Page 141
The inspiration for this bulto, *Infant Child, Flower of Mary* by Charles Carrillo, came from Mexican and Spanish paintings and Flemish prints from the Spanish Colonial period that depicted the Blessed Virgin Mary with a lily coming out of her belly. "This symbol always occurred in printed images, never in sculptures," says Carrillo.

Three bultos of Our Lady of the Harvest
by Marie Romero Cash.

The various advocations of Mary comprise the second category
of religious subjects for bultos. Of the many representations of the
Virgin Mary, Our Lady of Guadalupe is one of the most celebrated in
New Mexican art, states Félix López, because she is the protector of the
poor and marginalized people. Guadalupe performs not one, but several
miracles, which Thomas Steele summarizes in *Santos and Saints*:

> *Juan Diego, a recent Indian convert, was walking to mass
> in the early hours of 9 December 1531 when he heard singing from a
> bright cloud at a hill held sacred to Tonantzin, an Aztec goddess. A
> voice from the cloud summoned Juan Diego, and he saw a young
> woman whose brilliance made the brambles and rocks of the hilltop
> look like jewels. She identified herself as the Virgin Mary and*

*promised her help to the native peoples if the
bishop would build a chapel to her at the hill.*

*Juan Diego took her message to the
bishop as instructed, but the prelate disbelieved
his story. Juan reported to the lady that evening
on his way homeward; she asked him to try
again the next day, though Juan Diego suggested
that she send someone more influential than he.*

*At the next interview, the bishop
requested some sign, as Juan Diego reported to
the lady at a third apparition. She promised to
respond to the bishop, telling Juan Diego to
return the following morning.*

*But the young man had to spend the
whole of the next day tending his uncle, who
had fallen ill, and when the old man took a
turn for the worse during the night and seemed about to die, Juan
Diego set out at daybreak on 12 December to summon a priest to
administer the last rites of the Church. As he approached the hill, he
tried to skirt it as widely as possible so as to avoid the woman, but
she descended the hill to meet him. She assured him she had
appeared to his uncle and cured him, then she bade Juan Diego
climb to the top of the hill and pick the flowers he would find bloom-
ing there, and arranged them in his tilma when he returned to her.
He took them to the bishop, and when he loosened his tilma to drop
the flowers before him, the likeness of Our Lady of Guadalupe was
displayed upon it.*

**The Blessed Mother, Our Lady of the
Rosary, and St. Michael by Sabinita López
Ortiz. Another name for Our Lady of the
Rosary is *La Conquistadora*. The original
is a Spanish statue that was brought to
New Mexico in 1626, rescued during
the Pueblo Revolt, and returned to Santa
Fe after the reconquest. It resides in the
cathedral in Santa Fe and is a symbol
to Hispanic New Mexicans of their long
history in the Southwest. In 1992, La
Conquistadora was renamed Our Lady
of Peace.**

It is particularly significant that the Virgin Mary's only appearance in the
Americas occurred to an Indian, thus making her an object of veneration
to both Native American and Spanish people in this hemisphere.

Gustavo Victor Goler places his bulto of Nuestra Señora de
Guadalupe in a nicho within a three-dimensional frame that serves as a
backdrop for the narrative: Juan Diego opens his cloak to the kneeling
bishop, expecting to deliver the miracle of roses that the Virgin has made

bloom in the middle of December. Instead, he reveals the even greater miracle of Guadalupe's image on the inside of his garment (see page 143).

If Nuestra Señora de Guadalupe is the most pervasive image of the Virgin, Our Lady of the Harvest is the newest. Conceived by santera Marie Romero Cash, Our Lady of the Harvest is a nondenominational folk carving of the Virgin Mary as a nineteenth-century lady with high lace-up black boots and colorful dress. Her identity is apparent in the crescent moon—symbol of the Virgin—painted on the skirt of the middle figure, the crosses on the skirt and bodice of the other two figures, and the crowns (see page 144).

Angels constitute another category of art for bultos: the archangels St. Michael, St. Gabriel, and St. Raphael, and the guardian angels. San Miguel Arcángel (St. Michael the Archangel) is a favorite for both historic and contemporary santeros because he fights the devil and all his temptations. In Colonial New Mexico, the frontier was a dangerous place, full of unknown evils. Félix López delineates the traditional iconography for San Miguel: dressed for battle with a crown on his head, St. Michael wields his sword against the devil in one hand and holds scales in the other in which he weighs souls for their entrance into heaven.

Like St. Michael, St. Raphael was equally important to the colonizers. As Thomas Steele says: "Raphael is the guide of travelers and pilgrims and the source of spiritual and physical health. He is also a protector against monsters." Luisito Luján depicts the angel with his traditional attributes, holding a fish and a staff, but adds a sweetness of attitude. San Rafael is also the protector against blindness, and Luján portrays him with all-seeing eyes (see page 149).

§

Contemporary New Mexican santero art has burgeoned over the last thirty years, attracting collectors from all over the world. The art is characterized by innovations in style, use of new and old materials, refinement of techniques, and a breadth of vision. The artistic accomplishment of contemporary santeros is demonstrable. But what is most

St. Michael's dominance over evil is so complete that Félix López depicts the devil hiding and cringing beneath the angel's attack. The devil in this bulto is a separate sculpture that can be moved. Despite the tension of the battle, López does not forget San Miguel's true nature, evident in the beatific features of his face.

San Rafael by Luisito Luján. The translation of the Hebrew "Raphael" is "God Heals."

striking, perhaps, is how close the modern santeros remain to their predecessors in their actions and their visions.

Both historic and contemporary santeros base their art on conventional attributes of saints. The earliest historic santeros modeled their iconography after prints of religious art imported from Mexico. Contemporary santeros study historic bultos and retablos in museum collections and village churches, and many of them look at Mexican and European sources and analogues.

Historic and contemporary santeros generally use the same methods of construction in making bultos and retablos: they hand-adze the wood, prepare their own gesso, mix natural colors. Some varnish their bultos with piñon pitch. Most use woods native to northern New Mexico: cedar, pine, aspen, and cottonwood.

Like their predecessors, contemporary santeros make art for home altars, family chapels, and churches. Much of the art is donated; some is commissioned. The number of church commissions contemporary santeros have filled is noteworthy, illustrating that their role in the late twentieth century has now returned to that of the historic santeros. Nineteenth-century santeros went from village to village, filling commissions. José Rafael Aragón had an active workshop to fill his commissions.

Among historic and contemporary santeros are those adept at restoration. In the historic period, santeros were often called upon to repaint a fading altar screen or repair a broken bulto. In many instances, the santero simply painted over the work of his predecessor. Today, santeros spend months painstakingly removing surface dust and grime to reveal original surfaces below, which are restored and then protected against future damage.

Both historic and contemporary santeros are religious men and women who see their being santeros as a sacred role, in which the process of making a handcrafted work of art is an act of devotion. Félix López speaks for many of the santeros when he says, "I want the spirit of the image to be in my work, and I never forget that creating a santo is a *spiritual* process to be done with dignity and reverence."

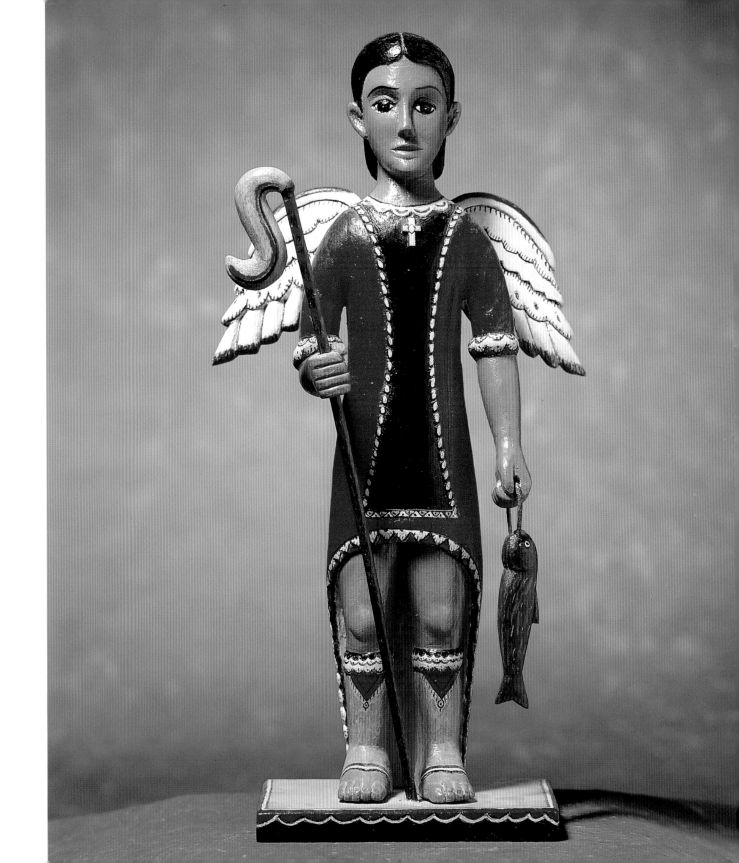

Glossary

Note: All foreign words are Spanish unless otherwise noted.

adobe: A brick or building material of sun-dried earth and straw.

adze: A cutting tool with an arched blade set at right angles to the handle, used for hewing wood into a smooth surface.

alacena: A wall cupboard generally covered with wooden doors.

andas: A wooden carrying litter.

aniline dye: A synthetic dye.

appliqué: The process of applying a cut-out decoration to another surface with glue, as in straw appliqué.

araña: Spider; also a wooden chandelier.

armario: A freestanding wardrobe, popularly called a *trastero* in New Mexico.

banco, banca: A bench. Also refers to the built-in banquette in adobe homes.

board chest: A chest in which the four sides are joined together with dovetail joints.

brazilwood: A dye that produces reds and purples, imported into New Mexico during the eighteenth and nineteenth centuries for the textile industry.

bulto: A three-dimensional religious sculpture, generally carved from wood.

caja: A storage chest; also a strong box used for cash and valuables.

Camino Real: The "king's highway." The primary thoroughfare and trade route from Mexico City north into the New Mexican frontier during the Spanish Colonial period.

campo santo: A cemetery.

candelero: A candlestick.

capilla: A chapel.

carpintero: A carpenter or woodworker.

carreta: A two-wheeled cart.

chamisa: The Spanish for rabbit brush, a plant that produces a yellow dye.

Chimayó weaving: The Chimayó weaving has a central pattern, usually a diamond or chevron motif, which is bordered on either end by horizontal bands. A repeating design motif often flanks the central form.

chip-carve: A method of incising designs into wood by making two parallel marks and chipping out the wood between them. Córdova wood carving is characterized by chip-carving.

churro: The breed of sheep brought to the New World by the Spanish. The wool's long straight fibers and low lanolin content make it an excellent wool for weaving.

cochineal: A red dye procured from the dried bodies of female cochineal insects that feed on the prickly pear cactus. Imported into New Mexico in the Spanish Colonial period.

cofradía: A confraternity, society, or guild.

colcha embroidery: A wool-on-wool or wool-on-cotton embroidery indigenous to New Mexico.

cota: Also known as Navajo tea, this plant produces a range of golds, oranges, and rust colors. It is also a popular tea.

criada: A servant; in Spanish households, this was often a Navajo woman assigned tasks of spinning and weaving.

Doña Sebastiana: The Hispanic New Mexican representation of Death as a female skeleton with a bow and arrow or a raised scythe, riding in her *carreta de muerte,* or death cart.

dovetail joint: The tenon (projecting tongue on a piece of wood) is flared and fit into a matching mortise (similarly shaped cavity in another piece of wood) to form a right-angle joint.

embossing: To raise a design in relief by punching from the reverse side of the metal.

encomienda: A system established by the Spanish Crown to collect tribute from the Pueblos in exchange for protection and religious instruction.

encrusting: The process of embedding cut-out straw into a piñon pitch glue applied heavily to a wooden surface and then sealing the design with a thinner mixture of the resin as a varnish.

entrada: An official expedition into a new territory.

"eyedazzler": A broad term for a style of Navajo blanket that evolved ca. 1875 and incorporates serrated diamond patterns influenced by the Saltillo sarape and Rio Grande weavings; it is also characterized by bright color combinations made possible with the introduction of synthetic dyes.

false framed chest: Strips of wood are applied to the exterior of a board chest to imitate a framed chest.

farol: A lantern.

framed chest: The panels of the chest fit into channels formed by vertical stiles and horizontal rails that are constructed with mortise-and-tenon joints.

frazada: A blanket.

Germantown yarn: Germantown, Pennsylvania (now included in Philadelphia), was a manufacturing center for commercially spun and synthetic-dyed yarn beginning in the mid 1860s.

gesso: *Yeso* is a native plaster, similar to plaster of paris, made by mixing gypsum with glue. Used by historic and contemporary santeros to cover the surface of wood before painting.

hacendado: Landowner.

harinero: A large chest for storing grain or flour.

hide painting: A religious painting on hide.

horno: A beehive-shaped adobe oven used to bake bread; introduced to the Pueblos by the Spanish and still in use today.

indigo: One of the most important dyes in the Spanish Colonial period, indigo was imported into New Mexico in lump form from New Spain. Indigo, or *añil,* yields a variety of blues.

jerga: A coarse woolen cloth, usually twill-woven with a plaid design, used as a floor covering, for clothing, and for packing material.

kiva: (Hopi). A ceremonial chamber within the Pueblo cultures, often built below the ground and entered from the top by a ladder.

La Muerte: An image of Death.

latilla: A small wooden pole laid diagonally across vigas to support the ceiling.

lunette: A half-moon design frequently placed at the top of retablos among other objects.

malacate: A hand spindle for spinning yarn.

manita: "Little hand." Also refers to the leaf motif found in Saltillo and Rio Grande weavings.

manta: A wearing blanket, wider than it is long, woven in cotton by the Pueblo Indians.

marquetry: A decorative process in which elaborate patterns are formed by inlaying pieces of wood, shell, or ivory into a wood veneer.

mestizo: A person of mixed blood; specifically a person of mixed European and American Indian ancestry.

monstrance: A holder used to expose the host of the Eucharist to the faithful for veneration.

morada: The meeting place or chapter house of the Penitente Brotherhood.

mordant: A chemical that fixes a dye.

mortise-and-tenon joint: A method of joining two pieces of wood, in which the tenon (a projecting tongue on one piece of wood) is cut to fit into the mortise (usually a rectangular-shaped cavity) to form a joint.

mosaic overlay: A technique of applying pre-cut materials to a surface with glue and then grinding them down to form one surface, which is then polished.

nicho: A recess in a wall, or a freestanding cabinet for statues.

obraje: A workshop.

oratorio: A family chapel or a private place, usually in the home, for prayer.

pantalla: A simple right-angle sconce.

Penitente: A member of a lay religious confraternity of Hispanic men, today recognized by the Catholic Church, and known as the Brothers of Our Father Jesus of Nazarene.

puddling: A technique of working a mixture of earth into a dense mass.

pueblo: Pueblo is Spanish for a town or a village. When the Spanish first explored the Southwest and encountered Native American cultures living in permanent villages, they referred to them as the Pueblos, or Pueblo peoples.

rag rug: A weaving composed of hundreds of fragments of cloth woven into strips.

repisa: A wall shelf.

reredos: An ornamental screen behind an altar with individual bays for paintings or sculptures. An Anglo-French word, the plural is reredoses.

retablo: A religious painting on a flat tablet of wood, usually pine. In the Spanish Colonial period, *retablo* also referred to altar screens.

Rio Grande weaving: The textiles produced by Hispanic weavers from the Spanish Colonial period through the end of the nineteenth century in New Mexican villages up and down the Rio Grande. The styles range from the pristine band-and-stripe designs to the highly sophisticated and complex designs influenced by the Saltillos.

sabanilla: A handspun wool sheeting material used as the foundation for colcha embroidery, as well as for clothing and mattress ticks.

Saltillo: Originated by the Tlaxcalan Indians in Mexico, this style of weaving reached its zenith in the eighteenth and nineteenth centuries. Characterized by a serrated central diamond or medallion motif, the background field of the Saltillo is filled with tiny repeating patterns; horizontal borders include further intricate patterns that complement the whole. The Saltillo is also distinguished by the fineness of its weave.

santero, santera: One who paints or carves images of saints. Also refers to the person who takes care of the *santos* (in a church, for example).

santo: A carved or painted image of a saint. The word also means "holy."

sarape: A woolen blanket with a slit in the middle for the head, worn over the body like a poncho.

scoring: Making a line with a sharp instrument on tin or other metals.

solder: A metal alloy that is melted to join two metal surfaces together.

splats: Thin vertical panels between the seat and top rail of a chair.

stamping: To imprint a design on a metal surface with a die.

stretcher: A horizontal wooden bar extending between the legs of a chair.

taller: A workshop or studio.

tapestry weave: A technique in which the image is formed by various colored, discontinuous wefts. Tapestry also refers to the fineness of a weave, made possible by spinning the yarn to a very thin diameter.

tarima: A stool.

terneplate: Sheet iron or steel coated with an alloy of tin and lead.

trastero: A tall cabinet used for storage, typically with a cut-out design on the upper portion of the doors.

treadle loom: Brought by the Spanish to the New World, the horizontal treadle loom is designed to store extensive lengths of warp on a horizontal warp beam. The treadles are foot pedals that manipulate the harnesses, separating individual warp threads from each other.

Vallero: A style of Hispanic weaving popularized by the Montoya sisters in El Valle in the late nineteenth century and characterized by strong colors, detailed vertical borders, and multiple eight-pointed stars.

vargueño: A writing desk that resembles a chest when closed; when open, the top drops down to reveal a writing platform and multiple compartments for writing tools. Also spelled *bargueño*.

vegetal dyes: Also called natural dyes, these are dyestuffs derived from plant material. Before 1860, when aniline, or synthetic, dyes were invented, natural dyes were the only dyes available.

viga: A ceiling beam.

Yei: (Navajo). The Yei are the Holy People of the Navajo, frequently portrayed in Hispanic as well as Navajo weaving.

Yerba de la víbora: Called snakeweed, this plant produces a bright yellow dye.

Bibliography

Awalt, Barbe, and Paul Rhetts. *Charlie Carrillo—Tradition & Soul/Tradición y Alma*. Albuquerque: LPD Press, 1995.

Baca, Elmo. *Rio Grande High Style Furniture Craftsmen*. Layton, Utah: Gibbs Smith, 1995.

Boyd, E. *Popular Arts of Spanish New Mexico*. Santa Fe: Museum of New Mexico Press, 1974.

Briggs, Charles L. *The Wood Carvers of Córdova, New Mexico*. Albuquerque: University of New Mexico Press, 1989. Original publication: University of Tennessee Press, 1980.

Cash, Marie Romero. *Built of Earth and Song*. Santa Fe: Red Crane Books, 1993.

Chávez, Fray Angélico. *My Penitente Land—Reflections on Spanish New Mexico*. Santa Fe: Museum of New Mexico Press, 1974. Revised, with an introduction by Thomas J. Steele, S.J., 1993.

Coulter, Lane, and Maurice Dixon. *New Mexican Tinwork—1840–1940*. Albuquerque: University of New Mexico Press, 1990.

Delaney, John J. *Pocket Dictionary of Saints*. New York: Doubleday, 1983.

Dickey, Roland F. *New Mexico Village Arts*. Albuquerque: University of New Mexico Press, 1949, 1970, 1990. All references are from the 1990 edition.

Fane, Diana, ed. *Converging Cultures—Art and Identity in Spanish America*. New York: The Brooklyn Museum in association with Harry N. Abrams, Inc., 1996.

Fisher, Nora, ed. *Rio Grande Textiles*. Santa Fe: Museum of New Mexico Press, 1994. This is a new edition of *Spanish Textile Tradition of New Mexico and Colorado*, 1979.

Forrest, Suzanne. *The Preservation of the Village—New Mexico's Hispanics and the New Deal*. Albuquerque: University of New Mexico Press, 1989.

Frank, Larry. *New Kingdom of the Saints—Religious Art of New Mexico, 1780–1907*. Santa Fe: Red Crane Books, 1992.

Gavin, Robin Farwell. *Traditional Arts of Spanish New Mexico*. Santa Fe: Museum of New Mexico Press, 1994.

Howard, Kathleen L., and Diana Pardue. *Inventing the Southwest—The Fred Harvey Company and Native American Art*. Flagstaff, Arizona: Northland Publishing, 1996.

Jenkins, Myra Ellen, and Albert H. Schroeder. *A Brief History of New Mexico*. Albuquerque: University of New Mexico Press, 1974.

Kalb, Laurie Beth. *Crafting Devotions—Tradition in Contemporary New Mexico Santos*. Albuquerque: University of New Mexico Press in association with Gene Autry Western Heritage Museum, 1994.

Kay, Elizabeth. *Chimayó Valley Traditions*. Santa Fe: Ancient City Press, 1987.

Mera, H. P. *Spanish-American Blanketry*. Santa Fe: School of American Research, 1987.

Pierce, Donna, and Marta Weigle, eds. *Spanish New Mexico*. 2 vols. Santa Fe: Museum of New Mexico Press, 1996.

Romero, Orlando, and David Larkin. *Adobe—Building and Living with Earth*. Boston: Houghton Mifflin, 1994.

Simmons, Marc. *The Last Conquistador—Juan de Oñate and the Settling of the Far Southwest*. Norman: University of Oklahoma Press, 1991.

Steele, S.J., Thomas J. *Santos and Saints—The Religious Folk Art of Hispanic New Mexico*. Santa Fe: Ancient City Press, 1994.

Taylor, Lonn, and Dessa Bokides. *New Mexican Furniture—1600–1940*. Santa Fe: Museum of New Mexico Press, 1987.

Usner, Don J. *Sabino's Map*. Santa Fe: Museum of New Mexico Press, 1995.

Vedder, Alan C. *Furniture of Spanish New Mexico*. Revised edition. Santa Fe: Sunstone Press, 1982.

Wakeley, David, and Thomas A. Drain. *A Sense of Mission—Historic Churches of the Southwest*. San Francisco: Chronicle Books, 1994.

Warren, Nancy Hunter. *Villages of Hispanic New Mexico*. Santa Fe: School of American Research, 1987.

Weber, David J. *The Spanish Frontier in North America*. New Haven: Yale University Press, 1992.

Weigle, Marta. *Brothers of Light, Brothers of Blood—The Penitentes of the Southwest*. Santa Fe: Ancient City Press, 1976.

———. *The Penitentes of the Southwest*. Santa Fe: Ancient City Press, 1970.

Weigle, Marta, and Barbara A. Babcock, eds. *The Great Southwest of the Fred Harvey Company and the Santa Fe Railway*. Phoenix: The Heard Museum, 1996.

Weigle, Marta, with Claudia Larcombe and Samuel Larcombe, eds. *Hispanic Arts and Ethnohistory in the Southwest*. Santa Fe: Ancient City Press, 1983.

Wroth, William. *Images of Penance, Images of Mercy—Southwestern Santos in the Late Nineteenth Century*. Norman: University of Oklahoma Press, 1991.

———, ed. *Furniture from the Hispanic Southwest*. Santa Fe: Ancient City Press, 1984.

Sources

Note: Each artist in the book received a questionnaire to complete on artistic questions and biographical information. In addition, personal and telephone interviews were conducted with the artists listed below from September 1996 to May 1997. Some earlier interviews were conducted in 1992. The interviews and questionnaires are the source for artists' quotes, information attributed to artists, and biographical background included in the text.

Artists interviewed

Antonio Archuleta
Delores Medina Archuleta
Eppie Archuleta
Teresa Archuleta-Sagel
Charles Carrillo
Marie Romero Cash
David C'de Baca
Cordelia Coronado
Greg Flores
Lydia García
Gustavo Victor Goler
María Fernández Graves
Monica Sosaya Halford
Rita Padilla Haufmann
Nicholas Herrera
Anita Romero Jones
Roberto Lavadie
Eurgencio López
Félix López
Fred Ray López
Gloria López
Irene López
José Benjamín López
Ramón José López
Abad Lucero
David Nabor Lucero
Luisito Luján
Agueda Martínez
Angelina Delgado Martínez
Karen Martínez
Norma Medina
Wilberto Miera
Robert Montoya
David Ortega

Eulogio and Zoraida Ortega
Sabinita López Ortiz
Alcario Otero
Lawrence Quintana
Mel Rivera
Paula and Eliseo Rodríguez
Vicki Rodríguez
Emilio and Senaida Romero
Fred Romero
Robert Romero
Charlie Sánchez
Leonard Salazar
Bonifacio Sandoval
Don Leon Sandoval
Arlene Cisneros Sena
Luis Tapia
Irvin Trujillo
Jimmy Trujillo
Lisa Trujillo
Johanna Terrazas
Horacio Valdez
María Vergara-Wilson

Introduction

PAGE

16. "He was the godfather...": Marc Simmons, *The Last Conquistador—Juan de Oñate and the Settling of the Far Southwest*, p. 195.

Chapter One

30. "Chimayó": Don J. Usner, *Sabino's Map*, p. 221.

30. Beginning of Ortega's Weaving Shop: David Ortega interview.

38. "large and very complex...": Joe Ben Wheat, "Saltillo Sarapes of Mexico," *Rio Grande Textiles*, p. 61.

39. "the New Mexican colcha...": E. Boyd, *Popular Arts of Spanish New Mexico*, p. 209–210.

42. "Spanish Wheel": Teresa Archuleta-Sagel, "Vallero Star Blankets," *Collectors Guide* (Albuquerque: Wingspread Inc.), Vol. 9, No. 1, 1995.

44. "We awoke to our...": Teresa Archuleta-Sagel, Introduction, *Rio Grande Textiles*, p. ix.

44. "historical context": Ibid, p. xi.

52. Description of preparing wool: Rita Padilla Haufmann interview.

53. Definition of tapestry weave: Teresa Archuleta-Sagel interview.

55. Vallero style woven by Trujillo family: Irvin Trujillo interview.

56. Description of "La Vereda": Ibid.

Chapter Two

60. Description of Las Trampas Church: Dr. Donna Pierce telephone interview.

77. "It is so...": David C'de Baca interview.

Chapter Three

80. "marquetry work...": Donna Pierce, "Straw Appliqué," *Spanish New Mexico*, Vol. 1, p. 83.

82. "artistic interface...": Ibid., p. 84.

83. "It's like a prayer...": Eliseo Rodríguez interview.

84. "poor man's gilding": E. Boyd, *Popular Arts of Spanish New Mexico*, p. 309.

90. Angelina Delgado Martínez interview.

90. "small quantities...": Lane Coulter and Maurice Dixon, *New Mexican Tinwork—1840–1940*, p. 3.

91. "encouraged the use...": Ibid., p. 3.

92. "Spanish craft stores...": Ibid., p. 141.

93. Information on terneplate: Angelina Delgado Martínez interview.

Chapter Four

108. Charles Carrillo: artist interview.

109. "the individualistic point of view...": Thomas J. Steele, S.J., *Santos and Saints*, p. 20.

110. "are referred to by...": Robin Farwell Gavin, *Traditional Arts of Spanish New Mexico*, p. 36–37.

114. "exorbitant fees...": Marta Weigle, *The Penitentes of the Southwest*, p. 5.

118. "procession of the Descent...": William Wroth, *Images of Penance, Images of Mercy*, p. 48.

118. "In Colonial New Mexico...": From an unpublished paper by Charles Carrillo.

119. "Between her son's...": *Santos and Saints*, p. 155.

122. "predicated upon...": Charles Briggs, *The Wood Carvers of Córdova, New Mexico*, p. 51.

124. "Freedom is probably...": Luis Tapia interview.

126. "Civil Rights Movement...": Charles Carrillo interview.

126. Carrillo, "This is the first time...": Taped interview.

127. "There were over...": Luis Tapia interview.

127. "Romantic Revival...": *Santos and Saints*, p. 125.

129. San Pascual background: Charles Carrillo interview.

129. "convention derived...": Roland Dickey, *New Mexico Village Arts*, p. 144.

129. Herrera, "social commentary...": Artist questionnaire.

132. "I paint...": Monica Sosaya Halford interview.

133. Ortega, "The chapel...": Artist questionnaire.

135. "My mother's car...": Luis Tapia interview.

136. "on a well-carved piece...": Charles Briggs, *The Wood Carvers of Córdova, New Mexico*, p. 167.

138. "the divine persons...": Thomas J. Steele, S.J., *Santos and Saints*, p. 41.

140. López, "I'm trying to learn...": Artist interview.

143. "This symbol...": Charles Carrillo telephone interview.

144. "Juan Diego,...": Thomas J. Steele, S.J., *Santos and Saints*, p. 63.

147. "Rafael is the guide...": Ibid., p. 157.

148. "I want the spirit...": Taken from questionnaire completed by Félix López.

Collection and Photograph Credits

(Note: All photography with the exception of archival shots, and as noted, is by Eric Swanson.)

Front Cover Art

From left to right: Courtesy Don Leon Sandoval. San Ysidro (retablo), by Belarmino Esquibel. L.5.96.1. Collection of the Spanish Colonial Arts Society, Inc., on loan to the Museum of New Mexico, Museum of International Folk Art. Courtesy of Vicki Rodríguez. Courtesy Chris Manzanares-Sandoval/Artisans of the Desert Inc.

Introduction

PAGE

2. Courtesy Mark and Lerin Winter.

4. Las Trampas, New Mexico, ca 1910. Photograph by Jesse Nusbaum. Courtesy Museum of New Mexico, #36466.

5. Top left: Courtesy Lisa R. Trujillo.
Top right: Detail, courtesy of Lawrence E. "Lorenzo" Quintana.
Bottom left: Courtesy Vicki Rodríguez.
Bottom right: Detail, Anonymous Private Collection.

14. Santuario de Chimayó, ca 1915-1917. Photograph by T. Harmon Parkhurst. Courtesy Museum of New Mexico, #13762.

15. Collection of Estrellita de Atocha Carrillo.

17. Mission at San Felipe Pueblo, 1899. Photograph by Adam C. Vroman. Courtesy Museum of New Mexico, #12370.

19. Bulto of Nuestra Señora de Carmen by José Rafael Aragón. Courtesy Museum of New Mexico, #59412.

20. Courtesy Bill and Barbara W. Douglas.

22. Courtesy Mr. and Mrs. Robert L. Clarke.

23. Bulto by José Dolores López. Courtesy Museum of New Mexico, #21274.

24. Bulto by Eurgencio López, Dewey Family Collection. Bultos by George López and José Mondragón, Taylor Museum of the Colorado Springs Fine Arts Center.

Chapter One

26. Courtesy Don Leon Sandoval.

27. Top: Courtesy Norma H. Medina. Bottom: Courtesy Agueda S. Martínez and Louisa García.

28. Top: Nicacio Ortega, Chimayó, New Mexico, 1958. Photograph by E.P. Haddon. Courtesy Museum of New Mexico, #151992. Bottom: Chimayó, New Mexico, 1911. Photograph by Jesse L. Nusbaum. Courtesy Museum of New Mexico, #13767.

29. Courtesy David Ortega.

30. Alvarado Hotel, Albuquerque, New Mexico, 1905. Photograph by G.W. Hance. Courtesy Museum of New Mexico, #66003.

31. Courtesy Tierra Wools Showroom, Los Ojos, New Mexico, and weavers Johanna M. Terrazas, Mary Velasquez, Sophie Martínez, and Nena Russom.

32. Anonymous Collection.

33. Jacobo O. "Jake" Trujillo. Courtesy Irvin and Lisa Trujillo.

34. Weaver, Chimayó, New Mexico, ca 1917. Courtesy Museum of New Mexico, #13770.

36. Courtesy Dewey Family Collection.

37. Courtesy Mark and Lerin Winter.

38. Anonymous Collection.

39. Courtesy Teresa Archuleta-Sagel.

40. Courtesy Delores Medina Archuleta.

41. The Albuquerque Museum.

42. Courtesy Mark and Lerin Winter.

43. Courtesy Ortiz Gallery.

45. Courtesy Lisa R. Trujillo.

46. Top left: Courtesy Dewey Family Collection.
Bottom right: Courtesy María Fernandez Graves.

47. Courtesy Eppie Archuleta.

48. Courtesy Louisa García.

50. Courtesy Teresa Archuleta-Sagel.

51. Rio Grande weaving, by Cordelia Coronado. FA.1990.21-1. Collection of the International Folk Art Foundation at the Museum of International Folk Art, Santa Fe.

52. Courtesy Rita Padilla Haufmann.

53. Courtesy Norma H. Medina.

54. Courtesy Joyce McMahon Hank.

55. Courtesy Irene E. López.

57. Courtesy Irvin L. Trujillo.

Chapter Two

58. Detail, courtesy Antonio J. Archuleta.

59. Top: Collection of El Rancho de las Golondrinas Museum.
Bottom: Carved chest, by George Sandoval. FA.87.363-1. Collection of the International Folk Art Foundation at the Museum of International Folk Art, Santa Fe.

61. Taos Pueblo North Side. Courtesy Museum of New Mexico #16707.

62. Courtesy Ray and Judy Dewey.

63. Governor Armijo's Room. Photograph by Ken Schar, Courtesy Museum of New Mexico, #58856.

64. Courtesy Ramón José López.

65. Courtesy Antonio J. Archuleta.

66. Spanish arm chair. Courtesy Museum of New Mexico, #26327.

67. Courtesy Antonio J. Archuleta.

68. Courtesy Greg Flores.

70. Courtesy Abad Lucero.

72. Courtesy Fred Romero.

73. Courtesy Wilberto Miera.

74. Top: Courtesy Lawrence E. "Lorenzo" Quintana.
Bottom: Photograph by Richard Kerlin. Collections of the Archdiocese of Santa Fe.

75. Courtesy Our Lady of Guadalupe Church, Taos.

76. Top left: Courtesy David E. C'de Baca.
Bottom left: Courtesy Tim Roybal.
Bottom right: Courtesy Federico Prudencio.
Top right: Courtesy Karen Martínez.

77. Courtesy David C'de Baca.

Chapter Three

78. Detail: Tin mirror with red and blue patterned inserts, by Angelina Delgado Martínez. Collection of the International Folk Art Foundation at the Museum of International Folk Art, Santa Fe.

79. Top: Courtesy Paula Rodríguez.
Bottom: Detail, courtesy Emilio and Senaida Romero.

80. Courtesy Eulogio Ortega and Zoraida G. Ortega.

81. Anonymous Private Collection.

83. Narrative cross, by Eliseo Rodríguez. A.86.565-2. Collection of the Museum of New Mexico at the Museum of International Folk Art, Santa Fe.

84. Courtesy Eliseo and Paula Rodríguez.

85. Courtesy Vicki Rodríguez.

86. Courtesy Frances Santiago de Murphy and Kevin Murphy.

87. Left: Taylor Museum of the Colorado Springs Fine Arts Center.
Right: Photograph by Michel Monteaux.

88. Collections of the Archdiocese of Santa Fe.

89. Courtesy Diane and Sandy Besser.

90. Federal style mirror and frame (with print of Juan Diego), courtesy Juan D. Martínez; framed mirror, courtesy Michael E. Griego; frame (with religious print), courtesy Jimmy Martin-Madrid.

91. Top: Courtesy Emilio and Senaida Romero.
Bottom: Anonymous Private Collection.

92. Francisco Delgado (1858-1936), tinsmith, Canyon Road, Santa Fe, New Mexico.

Photograph by T. Harmon Parkhurst. Courtesy Museum of New Mexico #71180.

93. Left: Tin frame by Eliseo Rodríguez. Courtesy Museum of New Mexico, #90210.
Right: Tin mirror with red and blue patterned inserts, by Angelina Delgado Martínez. Collection of the International Folk Art Foundation at the Museum of International Folk Art, Santa Fe.

94. Courtesy Fred Ray López.

95. Collection of Barbe Awalt and Paul Rhetts.

96. Tin altar with six bultos, by Anita Romero Jones. FA.87.161-1. Collection of the International Folk Art Foundation at the Museum of International Folk Art, Santa Fe.

97. Nicho with wallpaper inserts, courtesy Jimmy Martin-Madrid. Stamped tin nicho with statue of Santa Rita, courtesy Juan D. Martínez. Repisa with bulto of Our Lady of Sorrows by Robert M. Duran courtesy Michael E. Griego. Nicho with colcha inserts courtesy Donna Wright de Romero. Bulto of St. Isidore by Thomas L. Sena courtesy Bill and Barbara W. Douglas.

98. Courtesy Robert and Annie N. Romero.

99. Courtesy Bonifacio F. Sandoval.

100. Courtesy Emilio and Senaida Romero.

101. Right: The Albuquerque Museum.
Left: Courtesy Emilio and Senaida Romero.

Chapter Four

102. Detail, collection of Joseph L. Moure.

103. Top: Detail, Our Lady of Sorrows (bulto), by Gloria López Córdova. FA.1990.37-1. Collection of the International Folk Art Foundation at the Museum of International Folk Art, Santa Fe.
Bottom: Taylor Museum of the Colorado Springs Fine Arts Center.

105. San Ysidro (retablo), by Belarmino Esquibel. L.5.96.1. Collection of the Spanish Colonial Arts Society, Inc., on loan to the Museum of New Mexico, Museum of International Folk Art.

This bulto of San Ysidro Labrador by Ramón José López is mounted on an *andas*, or wooden carrying litter, and was made for the fiftieth anniversary of the Cristo Rey Church in Santa Fe. Parishioners carried the bulto to the Capilla de San Ysidro, a family chapel built by López's grandfather between 1929 and 1932 for his own private devotions (See page 104).

Index